Geography and Voting Behaviour

M. A. BUSTEED K

Theory and Practice in Geography

OXFORD UNIVERSITY PRESS · 1975

Oxford University Press, Ely House, London W. 1

GLASGOW NEW YORK TORONTO MELBOURNE WELLINGTON
CAPE TOWN IBADAN NAIROBI DAR ES SALAAM LUSAKA ADDIS ABABA
DELHI BOMBAY CALCUTTA MADRAS KARACHI LAHORE DACCA
KUALA LUMPUR SINGAPORE HONG KONG TOKYO

ISBN 0 19 874031 X

© Oxford University Press 1975

Printed in Great Britain
by J. W. Arrowsmith Ltd.,
Bristol.

Acknowledgements

This small book represents only an introduction to the rapidly developing field of electoral geography. The material and ideas have been drawn from a wide variety of sources too numerous to mention. However, there are several debts which must be acknowledged:
Professor J. W. House for his valuable comments on the original draft;
Mrs. Ellen Collier for typing the manuscript; P. J. Taylor and the Editor,
'Transactions of the Institute of British Geographers', for permission to
reproduce Figs. 4A and 4B; N. Deakin and the Pall Mall Press for reproduction of Fig. 10; and finally my wife, Helen, for drawing the maps
and diagrams.

Oxford, May 1975   M. A. Busteed

Contents

Introduction

Elections are confined to a relatively small number of states, mostly in north-west Europe, North America, and southern areas of Africa, Asia, and Australia. Most of the states concerned have a high level of economic and urban development and share significant elements of Anglo-American culture (Russett, 1967). In these cultural milieux socio-economic divisions are the most significant social cleavages and competition for power and influence is interpreted as competition for control over the means to organize, produce, and distribute economic wealth. Thus non-violent compromise and the use of elections and referenda are easy to accept because bargaining over such tangible, material elements as prices, wages, and working conditions is relatively easy. In states at a lower level of economic and urban development social cleavage is much more likely to be on the basis of religion, linguistic culture, or ethnic origin, and contrasts in wealth, income, and consumption more marked. Because of the non-material and emotional bases of many of these features comprise and consensus are much more difficult, with the result that elections are rare and violence is frequent. (Lipset, 1960).

There are also notable contrasts among those countries which do hold elections. Some of these variations may be due to differences in political history and tradition. Thus in the United Kingdom, where political life has usually been dominated by two major parties, and a simple, one-man one-vote system employed, the candidate with the largest number of votes in his constituency is the victor. In France, however, the historic multiplicity of parties led to a system whereby voting takes place in two rounds, usually seven days apart. In the first round candidates who gain a majority of votes over all others combined are declared elected. Where outright winners have not emerged, the two top candidates proceed to the second ballot. This is to guard against the election of a large number of representatives on minority votes. Such variations in electoral rules are commonplace, and in no way inhibit the academic study of electoral processes.

In many cases, however, where electoral law interferes seriously with the free expression of political preferences, academic study cannot have the same value. In the Soviet bloc countries of central and eastern Europe, and in several ex-colonial territories of eastern and south-central Africa, only one political party is permitted and all candidates must belong to it. Thus election results are not a legitimate expression of political opinion and the election campaign is not a fully open and free competition for office and power. Real changes and decisions are made elsewhere by different processes. Such an election may, in fact, be little more than an attempt to endow a regime with an air of democratic legitimacy. In these circumstances little can be usefully discussed beyond the level of turnout and perhaps the proportions of spoiled ballots. Prescott (1970) suggested that there were 71 countries where the elections were sufficiently open to repay detailed analysis and 57 where such efforts would be fruitless because of various constraints.

The general relationship between politics and geography is closer than has hitherto been realized. Modern governments have a profound effect on many aspects of their citizens' lives (Prescott, 1968). The activities of government have expanded considerably over the past hundred years, and now there are very few aspects of social, economic, and even artistic life totally untouched. This is certainly true of the economic and social geography of the state. Chisholm and Manners (1971) and Manners, Keble, Rodgers, and Warren (1972) have pointed out how, in Great Britain, government profoundly influences human geography. Significant elements of the national economy are in public ownership, so that decisions to run down some plants or industries and expand others can affect the lives of entire communities. Government decisions to expand higher education facilities involve the construction of new buildings, the employment of more teaching, administrative and maintenance staff, more accommodation for students, increased demand for local services, and the injection of increased spending power into the local economy (Chisholm and Manners, 1971). Decisions on the construction of new towns and cities lead to the creation of entirely new communities or the transformation of pre-existing settlements. Improvements in communications, and construction of motorways in particular, can transform the space relationships in a state, enhancing some locations and devaluing others.

There is also an increasing awareness of the impact of government decisions on the environment and much of the controversy surrounding the choice of a site for a third London Airport in the late 1960s and early 1970s grew out of fears about the loss of agricultural and scenic land, pollution by fumes and noise, and the likely growth in industry and population in the area chosen. Finally, many governments have adopted policies deliberately designed to steer economic activities away from some areas towards regions less fortunate in their economic structure. These policies can have notable effects on the over-all economic structure and the social and economic geography of a region (Busteed, 1974), and changes of government can sometimes lead to significant changes of emphasis. The return of a Conservative administration in July 1970 was followed by decisions to substitute tax allowances for direct grants to industry and to abolish the Regional Employment Premium (Chapman, 1971).

Geography is particularly important in that it can add an entirely new dimension to the study of elections. The geographer brings a characteristic emphasis on spatial location, distribution, and spatial interrelationships to the study of electoral behaviour, aspects not normally considered by other disciplines. In turn geography can benefit from electoral studies, through a deeper understanding of the processes and patterns underlying human behaviour in space. Finally, by the very nature of his subject, the geographer is probably the best equipped of all to undertake the delicate task of subdividing a state area into precisely delimited electoral districts for purposes of representation.

1 The spatial organization of electoral areas

Introduction

With a very few exceptions such as Israel, every state that holds popular elections is internally subdivided for purposes of representation. Individuals elected to public office may represent particular parties or groups, or may possess notable personal philosophies. However, they also represent areas known variously as constituencies, wards, districts, or, in a federal system, states, provinces, or regions. In most cases each area has one representative but where a system of proportional representation is used for voting there are multi-member constituencies, e.g. the Irish Republic.

If elected members represent a territory, then a structure of carefully delimited and defined areas and boundaries covering the entire national space must be devised. Precise definition of the areas and boundaries is necessary for various reasons. The spatial structure of local party groups is organized to coincide with the structure of areas and boundaries devised for representation, and, to avoid confusion, electors, elected representatives, and party workers must know precisely where the ward or constituency boundaries are.

The significance of any spatial structure of representative areas goes beyond mere administrative and organizational convenience. The way in which the boundaries are drawn can decide the result in an election. In some cases it is even possible to partition space so that, though a party wins a minority of votes, it gains a controlling majority of seats. However, boundaries may be drawn for other reasons besides partisan advantage. The organization of electoral areas, like many other aspects of elections, reflects the different history, traditions and political systems of individual states. A close examination of the British system of delimiting parliamentary constituencies serves to illustrate the way in which the final structure of areas and boundaries is arrived at, and also how such structures are rooted in the political culture of a state.

The British system of parliamentary elections

The British parliament at Westminster in 1974 comprised 635 members, each representing a territorially defined constituency. Over the past 150 years there has been a steady widening of the franchise, until by the early 1970s every adult aged 18 or over could vote, apart from members of the Royal Family, peers, lunatics, or convicted felons. This extension of the franchise was in large part a response to pressures for equality of political rights between all sections of the population. As part of the same idea there were demands for equality in the representation of population and areas. It was argued that it was immoral for small population centres, such as Canterbury, with 3868 electors at the 1906 election, to have the same representation as Romford which had over 45 000 voters, since this would render a vote in Canterbury worth 11½ votes in Romford. As a result, the allocation of seats throughout the country has been regularly reviewed and, if necessary, readjusted to accord more closely with the changing spatial distribution of electors.

Current procedure in the United Kingdom largely follows the recommendations of the Speaker's Conference on Electoral Reform in 1944. When reviews are conducted there are four boundary commissions, one each for England, Wales, Scotland, and Northern Ireland. Each consists of three members, and each is chaired by the Speaker of the Commons at Westminster. It is customary for such reviews to be conducted at least once every fifteen years. Evidence and proposals may be submitted to the commissioners by interested groups or persons, and on the basis of this and work they themselves may authorize, their recommendations on areas and boundaries are presented in Bills to Parliament. After discussion and possible amendment the Bill may become an Act and new constituencies adopted as a territorial basis for the next general election (Butler, 1955).

Clearly the principles upon which delimitation is based will determine the spatial structure which emerges. The British boundary commissions work to a fairly simple set of guidelines. First, they are constrained by the fact that the total number of parliamentary seats should be about 630. Second, as far as is practicable, the total number of electors in each seat should not be much greater or less than the electoral quota. This is calculated by dividing the total electorate in the U.K. by the total number of seats to be distributed. At the redistribution of seats in 1971 the number of M.Ps. was increased by five to 635, and the quota at the general election in February 1974 was 62 675 electors. However, this is not applied with equal rigidity throughout the country, for the number of seats allocated to Scotland and Wales is never less than 71 and 35 respectively, and Northern Ireland always has 12. On a strict application of the February 1974 quota, Scotland would have had 58 seats, Wales 31, and Northern Ireland 17. The reasons for these deviations are varied. It is possible that Scotland and Wales are allowed to be over-represented out of fear that a loss of seats might provoke a nationalistic reaction.

Northern Ireland is under-represented because the regional legislature at Stormont dealt with many matters which otherwise would have been the concern of Westminster. Thus Northern Irish M.Ps. have larger constituencies to make up the constituency work-loads.

Further guidelines are provided and deviations permitted when it comes to delimitation of boundaries. Variations of 25 per cent above and below the quota are traditionally permitted in remote rural and densely populated urban areas respectively because of the geography of population and communications. The total population in rural areas such as central Wales and northern Scotland is so sparse and so scattered that any attempt to delimit seats under strict application of the quota would result in constituencies so large in area that the task of travelling around to campaign or to contact constituents would be enormous. Equally, in some urban areas population is spatially so concentrated that campaigning and consultation are simplified.

As far as possible constituency boundaries in Britain must respect local government boundaries. This is rooted in the further principle that seats should be recognizable community areas, a consideration which is also taken into account when local authority areas are constructed. It is unusual to find markedly rural and urban areas combined within a single seat, and rural local authority boundaries are not often bisected by constituency boundaries. This is because of the desire to preserve community of interests wherever possible.

However, such carefully contrived structures are inevitably rendered obsolete by changes in economic and social geography and the accompanying migration. During the present century remote rural and central city areas of the U.K. have steadily lost population, while suburban areas surrounding large towns, particularly in central and south-eastern England, have gained notably. The inevitable result has been to render the existing scheme of constituency areas and boundaries obsolete. The task of the boundary commissions is to bring the spatial pattern of constituencies more into accord with the pattern of population and thereby ensure greater equality of representation.

The situation in the Manchester area since the mid 1950s is a good example of these interrelated changes. As a result of the redistribution which preceded the general election of 1955, Manchester County Borough had nine seats with a mean electorate of 57 286 and standard deviation of 4697. During the following 15 years, however, there were considerable population changes. By the General Election of 1970, all save two seats had lost electors, but particularly Ardwick, (− 32·8 per cent since 1955), Cheetham (− 42·7 per cent) and Exchange (− 59·8 per cent.). The mean electorate was now 49 220 and standard deviation had grown to 16 155. If the electorate of the entire city had been allocated representation on the basis of one member for 21 080 as in Exchange, then there would have been 21 Manchester M.P.s. instead of nine. Alternatively one per 78 036 as at Withenshawe would have yielded six members. Clearly a vote in Cheetham, Ardwick and Exchange had more political weight than one in Blackley, Gorton or Wythenshawe. A further difficulty arose over members' work-loads. Even allowing for the distinctive problems generated by inner urban areas such as Cheetham and Exchange, it is clear that there would be much more work involved in maintaining contact and dealing with the problems of an electorate almost four times as great as in Wythenshawe or Gorton.

Reorganization was therefore necessary, to ensure both equality of representation for electors and equality of work-load for members. The result of the 1973 redistribution was to reduce the city's parliamentary representation by one seat to eight M.Ps. Most of Cheetham and Exchange were amalgamated to form Manchester Central and small areas were distributed among surrounding constituencies (Fig. 1). The outcome was a more even distribution of electors with less variation between seats. The mean electorate became 50 295 and the standard deviation was reduced to 6207.

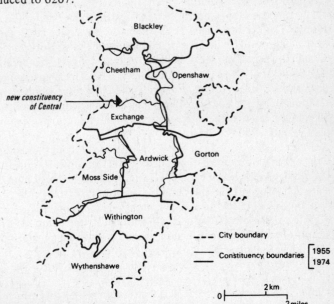

FIG. 1 Manchester constituency boundaries: 1955 and 1974 general elections

Organization of space for partisan ends

Unfortunately the delimitation of boundaries is not always carried out with the high-mindedness of the British boundary commissioners. It is by no means unknown for lines to be drawn in such a way as to maximize the electoral impact of support for one party and diminish that for another. The practice has become known as gerrymandering, after Governor Elbridge Gerry of Massachusetts who signed a districting law in 1812 which produced a pattern of constituencies reminiscent of the shape of a salamander. To carry out such a partisan drawing of boundaries clearly necessitates a detailed knowledge of local electoral geography. Such information is usually available only from local party workers and agents.

A common form of gerrymandering is for boundaries to be drawn in such a way that the strength of the opposition party is concentrated into one or two areas. In this way they will gain a few seats, but in so doing they accumulate a large and electorally useless surplus of votes in a few strongholds. The rest of the area may be safely subdivided in the knowledge that opposition strength has been harmlessly confined. This approach is difficult to detect from the map of electoral areas and boundaries alone. Its effects emerge most clearly when the election results are scrutinized, since it usually leads to a situation where a party's strength is overwhelmingly concentrated in one or two seats with massive majorities.

Before the County Borough was suspended in November 1968, the local government ward boundaries of Londonderry city in Northern Ireland had long been regarded as a classic example of gerrymandering. Certainly the results of the 1961 census and the 1967 local government elections provided strong *prima facie* evidence. The census recorded 18 432 Roman Catholic and 11 340 persons of other religious groups. It was generally agreed that the ratepayer franchise produced an electorate of approximately 7900 Protestants and 10 000 Catholics. In view of the deep-seated sectarian cleavage in Northern Irish society and the rigidity of voting behaviour, a Council controlled by the local Irish Nationalist Party would have appeared inevitable. However, since the ward boundaries were delimited in 1936 the Coundil had been Protestant and Unionist-controlled. In the Local Government elections of 1967 14 429 Nationalist votes produced eight Nationalist councillors. 8781 Unionist votes produced twelve Unionists, and a controlling majority. Careful examination of details at the ward level reveals that the Nationalist strength was overwhelmingly concentrated in North Ward, where they polled 10 047 votes, as against 1138 for the Unionists. This represented 69·6 per cent of total Nationalist voting strength of the

City and returned all the eight Nationalist representatives. In Waterside Ward which had four councillors, there was a small Unionist majority, and in North Ward, which returned eight councillors, the Unionist majority was equally small (Table 1).

TABLE 1

Londonderry County Borough. 1967 local election results.

	Nationalist votes	Unionist votes	Councillors elected
North Ward	2 530	3 946	8 Unionists
Waterside Ward	1 852	3 697	4 Unionists
South Ward	10 047	1 138	8 Nationalists
TOTAL	14 429	8 781	20

Detailed scrutiny of the ward boundaries and 1961 census returns reveals what these results suggest, namely that South Ward was almost entirely populated by Catholics and the remaining two wards strongly Protestant. While it is clearly impossible to prove conclusively that the original delimitation was carried out with this aim in mind, the end result was clearly anomalous.

An alternative approach to such electoral manipulation is to aim at concentration and maximum impact of one's own supporters. It is not infrequent to find that supporters of a particular political viewpoint are spatially scattered to such an extent that they are not sufficiently strong anywhere to elect a representative. In such cases it is possible to manipulate electoral boundaries to bring these electors into a single district where they are in a majority and can return the representative they desire. Two features are characteristic of the practice: first, the majority for the victor is usually rather small; second and much more marked, such manipulated districts have a characteristic shape. They are usually long and sinuous, with many curious salients and embayments, as they seek to bring the scattered pockets of voters together and avoid concentrations of opponents.

Until the Supreme Court decisions of *Baker* v. *Carr* (1962) and *Reynolds* v. *Simms* (1964) declared them unconstitutional, these practices were most widespread in the United States. It was for long an acknowledged fact that one of the fruits of a party's victory in state elections was the opportunity to redraw electoral boundaries, to derive the maximum impact from its own supporters and ensure continuation in office. The most intriguing shapes date from before the Supreme Court's pronouncements. The Ohio State Assembly had traditionally been Republican, thanks to the Party's strength in rural and small town districts and the over-representation of these areas. The city of Cleveland in Cuyahoga County, however, is strongly Democratic. The district boundaries in Cleveland used for the elections to the 87th Congress in 1960 (Fig. 2A) were so curious, particularly for district 23, that

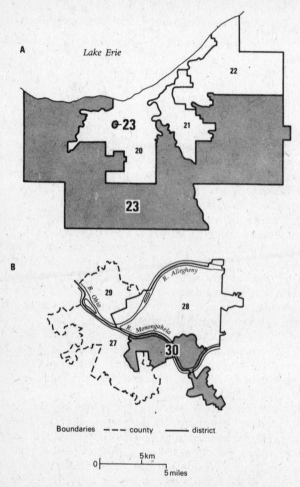

FIG. 2 U.S.A.: Congressional district boundaries for the 87th Congress (1960)
    A. Cleveland, Ohio
    B. Pittsburgh, Pennsylvania

it seems clear that there was a conscious attempt to concentrate the Republican strength. A similar situation seems apparent in the case of the 30th District for Pittsburgh, Pennsylvania (Fig. 2B).

A further method of manipulation involves dilution of an opponent's strength. This involves the careful drawing of boundaries to ensure that the opposition stronghold is divided up amongst several districts. Each area of opposition support is combined with an area where one's own supporters are more numerous. The difficulty about such a device is that once again it is frequently necessary to draw out the district boundaries over long distances to ensure that a sufficiently large number of one's own supporters have been included. There are three characteristic features of this approach: if a detailed breakdown of results is available, the supporters of the various parties are usually to be concentrated in distinct areas, with little or no inter-mixing; once again districts may be long and sinuous as the most favourable partisan balance is sought out; finally, it usually emerges that one party has far fewer representatives than its share of the votes would merit.

One of the best examples of this particular approach is provided by the recent history of Congressional districting in the American state of North Carolina. Like most of the States in the south-east of the U.S.A. until the late 1960s, North Carolina's politics were dominated by conservative Democrats, who normally command an overwhelming majority of the State and Congressional seats at elections. However, there were traditional areas of Republican strength in the more upland western and south-western parts of the state. In 1960 these were sufficiently numerous to gain almost two-fifths of the vote at the Congressional elections, but they only captured one of the State's twelve Congressional seats. This meant that it required 515 488 Republican votes to elect a Republican congressman and 71 543 to elect a Democrat. Examination of the spatial pattern of boundaries and areas gives a strong hint of how this came about (Fig. 3A.). Several of the Congressional districts, particularly in the western area, were long and sinuous, stretching a considerable distance across the State area. This was particularly true of districts 4, 5, 8, 9, 10, and 11. All of these contained pockets of Republican strength, but only in the Tenth district was this sufficient for victory. In the others the shape of the district plus the pattern of county victories in the election suggests the Democrat-dominated State Assembly has gone to considerable pains to ensure that Republican areas were combined with stronger Democratic areas. The effects of the redistricting initiated by the Supreme Court decisions of 1962 and 1964 may be gauged from the pattern of

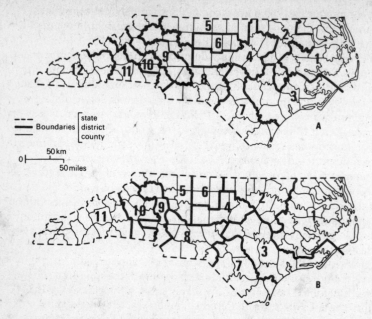

FIG. 3 Congressional district boundaries of North Carolina
A. For the elections to the 87th Congress (1960)
B For the elections to the 92nd Congress (1972)

Congressional districts and the election results of November 1970 for the 92nd Congress. The state lost one of its Congressional representatives and had the district boundaries redrawn because of population changes (Fig. 3B). Save for the Ninth and Tenth districts the new areas were much more compact than previously. The election results confirm the impression of a much fairer spatial structure. This time, in a year in which the Republicans were not doing particularly well, they won four of the eleven seats. Moreover, the Democrats now got one seat for 73 415 votes and the Republican got one for 102 685 votes, a much more equitable situation than in 1960.

It is also possible to increase the representation of a party by the practice of weighted representation. This involves allocating to certain districts more representatives than they would normally acquire under a strict application of the electoral quota. There may be perfectly plausible reasons behind such weighting. In many countries it is the custom to give exaggerated representation to rural areas, on the grounds that their

agricultural and small town interests are of vital significance to the
state and should be protected against the overwhelmingly larger populations and voting power of the urban and industrial areas. The factors
of population geography and travelling time, considered by British
boundary commissioners, also apply. These lines of reasoning are accepted
as the basis for inflated rural representation in states as diverse as the
U.S.A. (at federal and state level), France, the Republic of South Africa,
and the Republic of Ireland. However, whatever the original reasoning,
if the regions in question tend to give particularly strong support to one
party the end result is to increase the representation of that party. In the
U.S.A. the Republican Party and in South Africa the Afrikaaner
National Party have traditionally been the beneficiaries of rural weighting.
In France the Communists and socialists have suffered most from the
under-representation of urban areas.

One of the most notable examples of this practice has been provided
by the Irish Republic. The Irish Parliament, Dail Eireann, comprises 144
deputies elected from multi-member constituencies by the proportional
representation system known as the single transferable vote (Chubb,
1970). The Irish constitution states that as far as practicable the ratio
between deputies and population should be the same in every constituency throughout the country. In practice, however, this has never been
achieved. Three factors tend to work against equalization. The first is
migration. Throughout most of the present century the north-western
areas of Ireland have lost population at a rapid rate. Between the census
reports of 1966 and 1971 all eight of the counties which lost population
were in this area. The most notable population gains were in the Dublin
region, particularly the outer areas of the city and the surrounding
districts. Most of these gained at least 6 per cent in 1966–71 (Parker,
1972). Clearly this tends to erode any effort to preserve equality between
constituency populations, and constant readjustment is necessary. However two further factors tend to check this process. One is the argument
already encountered in the British context, that remote rural areas with
a scattered settlement pattern, demand a high expenditure of time for
campaign travelling and general constituency care. The second concerns
the national significance attached to these western areas, where elements
of the original Gaelic rural Ireland have survived longest and in least
modified form. Here are found most of the officially designated
Gaeltacht areas containing a high proportion of people who speak Irish
as their first language. The small family farm depending exclusively on
family labour is still the most significant element in the overwhelmingly
agricultural economy of the region. Starting at the turn of the century

the Irish nationalist movement harked back to these elements in Irish cultural traditions, and its programme included revitalization of the language and encouragement of the associated cultural milieu. Consequently these areas have always had a powerful nationalistic appeal in Irish politics, and it is argued that they should receive greater representation in the Dail than a strict application of the population ratio would allow, in order to defend their interests, which are those of true Ireland. This has in fact been the practice for some time.

The over-representation of the western areas has produced a corresponding under-representation of the eastern areas. At the census of 1971 the mean population per member in the Irish Republic was 20 635. On this basis the nine counties of the north-west of Ireland, with a total population of 692 699, deserved 33 members. In fact they had 36, giving a regional mean of 19 241 persons per representative. At the same census the constituencies of Dublin city, Dublin County, and Dun Laoghaire-Rathdown, with a total population of 852 219, deserved 41 seats if a national mean were applied. In fact they had only 38, making a regional mean of 22 426 persons per member. In party terms the result is to give at least two, if not three extra seats to Fianna Fail, the party which has governed Ireland for almost two-thirds of its existence as an independent state, and conversely to deprive its opponents of at least two seats. This situation reflects the electoral geography of the Irish Republic. The western areas are traditionally strong in support of Fianna Fail, usually giving the party well over half their first-preference votes. In the eastern urban areas, however, it is chronically weak and the Fine Gael and Labour parties are in a strong position (Busteed and Mason, 1974). Superficially it may seem that these few seats are of little importance, but in Irish politics they are vital. The proportional representation system has traditionally produced tiny majorities of one or two in the Irish parliament. Consequently, such careful weighting of representation can make the difference between forming a government or being relegated to the Opposition benches.

Non-partisan districting

The drawing of completely unbiased electoral districts is an extremely difficult task, best illustrated by reference to British and American experience. In both countries a fairly strict set of guidelines has been laid down to govern the redrawing of boundaries, although the mere establishment of criteria does not necessarily guarantee fairness or expedite the process of redistricting. The work of the British boundary commissioners has long been regarded as an example of unbiased delimitation. Certainly, it has never been seriously suggested that the commissioners intentionally set out to give an advantage to one party or to prevent fair representation of another. However, while the procedure of the commissioners and the over-all principles they work to are well known, almost nothing is known of the way in which they arrive at their final decisions. In particular it would be instructive to discover how they reconcile conflicting evidence and decide between the competing sets of equally legitimate schemes which must occasionally be presented to them. Allen (1964) suggested that in making their decisions the commissioners might be unduly influenced by arguments which would tend to preserve the social homogeneity of middle class and favour Conservative constituencies, because the middle class are more articulate in the presentation of arguments, and in addition 'the Commissioners themselves are likely to feel more affinity with representations of professional people in dark suits' (p. 191). He offered this to explain why some middle-class Conservative seats survived successive redistributions, despite their declining populations, while 'it does appear that the working class areas are treated more cavalierly, as if their views are of lesser account' (p. 191).

The exaggerated representation given in certain regions and districts is also open to criticism. In the United Kingdom, Scotland, Wales, and rural areas are over-represented. Whatever the principles behind the extra seats for Scotland and Wales, the result in both cases is a greater gain for the Labour Party than any other, since Labour usually hold at least three-quarters of the Welsh seats and about two-thirds of those in Scotland. Equally, the English rural areas are overwhelmingly Conservative, so that the allocation of extra seats to rural areas on the grounds of convenience and special interest may well mean greater Conservative representation. In the United States the under-representation of urban areas operated against ethnic groups and the Democrats, while the over-representation of rural areas favoured the Republicans.

However, equality of population totals between constituencies could not by itself guarantee fairness in electoral boundaries. It was a case of gross under-representation of urban voters in Tennessee which precipitated the famous U.S. Supreme Court ruling in the *Baker* v. *Carr* case. In various subsequent decisions the Court laid particular emphasis on the need for the number of inhabitants per legislator in one district to be substantially equal to the number of inhabitants per legislator in the other districts in the same state. These decisions initiated a frantic burst of redistricting activity, (Silva, 1965, Bushman and Stanley, 1971), designed to bring state and Congressional districts into line with changing population patterns and the Court's requirements. More-over, since these decisions, each state has been required to redistrict if the publication of the U.S. Census Returns reveals that notable changes in population patterns have upset the equality of representation. Experience has shown however, that the criterion of population equality alone does not produce a fair scheme. In Iowa the results of the 1970 census necessitated the reduction of the state's Congressional representation from seven to six and the redrawing of district boundaries. A group of local Republicans produced a scheme in which five districts had exactly equal populations of 470 840 and the sixth had only one more person. This met the Supreme Court's criterion to the letter, but was a violation in spirit since the scheme was widely recognized as a gerrymander which would concentrate all the Democratic strength into a single district and leave the remaining five safely Republican. (P.J. Taylor, 1973). Only detailed knowledge of local electoral geography and the shape of the proposed districts gave any clues about the underlying intention (Fig. 4A).

The fate of new redistribution schemes is often at the mercy of the government of the day. In the United States experience has shown that the Supreme Court can indicate both the criteria to be used and the timing of any scheme. In the United Kingdom timing remains in the hands of the incumbent government and recent experience suggests that this can be dictated by political circumstances. When any new structure of seats has been devised the recommendations are presented to the government of the day, which lays them before the House of Commons. After discussion and debate, during which the proposed boundaries may well be altered, the proposals are voted on. They are normally passed into law and the next general election is fought on the new constituency boundaries. Under British law this process must take place at least once every fifteen years. A redistribution was therefore due before the 1970 general election. However, since it is widely believed in British politics that Labour tends to lose seats as a result of redistribution, the incumbent Labour Government was most unhappy about the proposed changes, especially since some workers estimated that they would lose about 15 seats. Consequently the Government took the unique step of placing the Commissioners' recommendations before Parliament and instructing their supporters to vote them down. This they did, and the 1970 general election was fought on the old boundaries, first delimited in 1954. The reason given was that local government areas were also under review and since, as noted earlier, it is usual for these boundaries to coincide as far as possible with constituency boundaries, it was argued that redistribution should be postponed until the new pattern

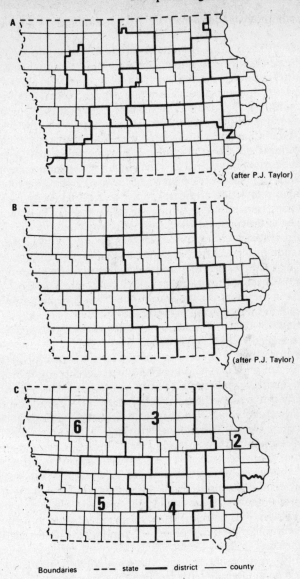

(after P.J. Taylor)

(after P.J. Taylor)

Boundaries   - - - state   —— district   —— county

0   50 km
    50 miles

FIG. 4 Iowa congessional districts
    A. The Republican proposals
    B. Taylor's bipartisan proposals
    C. The final boundaries

of local authorities was decided. The redistribution finally took place in 1973.

Another difficulty arises from the sheer size of the problem involved and the time consumed in evaluating the representative areas and boundaries of entire countries, judging their fairness or otherwise, and then drawing up and choosing between new alternative schemes. Haggett (1969) pointed out that in the closely similar, though smaller, problem of restructuring English local government in the late 1960s, the Redcliffe-Maud Commission were faced with 124 existing counties and county boroughs and the total number of possible combinations ran into 'hundreds of billions' (p. 216). The boundary commissioners for England during the same period were faced with 511 parliamentary seats. A rapid completion of the task of redrawing is necessary for two reasons. First, population geography seems to be changing at an accelerating rate, with the result that inequality of representation soon reappears, particularly in suburban areas. Approximately 15 per cent of the population of the U.S.A. changes residence annually, and it has been estimated that most legislative districts in America change by about 1 or 2 per cent while redistricting is being carried out (Morrill, 1973). Secondly, in some countries, particularly the U.S.A., the frequency of elections requires that revision of boundaries should be as swift as possible, otherwise there would be a succession of contests using boundaires which are increasingly inequitable.

A final difficulty is that a large proportion of the seats which are set up are safe for one party or another and it is argued that the electorate is denied a genuinely open contest and a democratic choice in such seats. Clearly this is a debatable point. Certainly in the United Kingdom there are many seats which could be regarded as safe and comparatively few which are marginal. This, it is generally agreed, is purely a non-intentional result of the way in which boundaries are drawn, rather than a conscious gerrymander. Moreover, some would argue that the continuity of personnel and experience provided by safe seats is valuable.

In view of all these considerations it is understandable that the U.S. Supreme Court's decisions stimulated considerable experimentation with the application of various types of computer program to redistricting problems. So far these computer programs have been applied much more widely in the U.S.A. (Vale, 1969), but there would seem to be scope for their use in the British context also (Mills, 1967, Cope, 1970). Their advantage lies in the fact that they are capable of scanning a mass of data, making rapid comparisons of alternative combinations of districts, and selecting the most satisfactory solution in accordance

with the selected criteria. These criteria may be selected to ignore such
considerations as weighting for particular areas or partisan advantage.

Four main methods have been used in computer redistricting (Vale,
1969). The Kaiser-Nagel method (Nagel, 1965) appeals to many
incumbent politicians and members of political organizations because
it starts with the existing electoral areas and disturbs them as little as
possible. The chief aim is to achieve equality of population. Thus it
begins with the core area of each district and adds or subtracts peripheral
districts until all have met the required standard of population equality.
However, it is clearly of little use when entirely new electoral areas are
required. The Weaver-Hess (1963) method requires first the identification of the major population centres. It then proceeds by adding
contiguous areas to these centres in accordance with preselected criteria,
until the prescribed population level is reached. Clearly this is much more
useful when entirely new areas are being formed. Furthermore it mini-
mizes the length of the perimeter, thereby making the creation of long,
sinuous, gerrymandered areas almost impossible. Also, by attaching
territory to urban centres, it recognizes the basic nature of service
relationships in modern social geography. The Forrest method (1965)
is the simplest and most purely mechanical of all. A master data tape for
a state or region is fed into the computer and the area and population
are analysed and broken down into rectangular areas of an equal population size previously chosen. Contiguity and population equality are
the only criteria observed. Such social considerations as community
areas are ignored and for some this is a disadvantage. The Hale-Whitney
(Hale, 1965) method is the most complex. At the heart of an urban area
a perfectly circular district is drawn, enclosing a predetermined electoral
quota. From its midpoint a ray of required radius is rotated clockwise to
describe a circle whose perimeter where possible follows existing county
lines. Each sector is a constituency and each contains an equal population.
The advantages claimed for this rather more complex program are many.
First, if the urban area is not too large, each constituency will contain
a social mixture of central urban, suburban, and rural areas, thereby
making it safe for no party, enhancing competition, and encouraging
public interest. Secondly, it acknowledges the fact that many modern
urban centres have tended to grow outwards along radial routes. But it
has the drawback that the areas are not compact, and though the city
may have grown along radial routes, it does not follow that community
areas have also organized themselves in sectors.

P.J. Taylor (1973) has suggested that the Kaiser-Nagel method may
be used in what he calls 'gerrymandering in reverse' designed to ensure

that the maximum number of seats possible are marginal and experience a genuine contest at election times. This could be achieved if those responsible for redistricting included bipartisan districts as one of their criteria and included the votes for the competing parties at recent elections amongst the data that they considered for manipulation. In this way it would be possible to ensure that a party received the same proportion of seats as of votes. Using these criteria Taylor suggested a new structure of bipartisan Congressional districts for Iowa (Fig. 4B) which may usefully be compared with an attempted Republican gerrymander (Fig. 4B) and the scheme actually adopted for the 1972 Congressional elections (Fig. 4C).

Unfortunately the experience of at least one professional geographer suggests that practical considerations weigh against ideal solutions to districting problems. After the results of the 1970 U.S. Census it became necessary to revise the state and federal district boundaries of the state of Washington. The Democrat-controlled State Senate produced a scheme of new districts which would have maintained and extended their Senate control, and the Republican-controlled lower house produced a scheme which would have tightened their grip on the House of Representatives and given them the Senate also. Under legal duress the parties attempted a compromise, but were unable to agree over new districts for the urban centres of Seattle and Spokane. To break the deadlock the Federal District Court in Seattle appointed the geographer Richard Morrill as 'Special Master' with the task of drawing up a new scheme of districts. As part of this he was given several criteria in order of priority (Morrill, 1973). As far as possible each district had to have a total population of 68 495, with a maximum possible deviation of 1 per cent, i.e. 685 persons. There was to be no subdivision of counties, cities, or census tracts; the new districts were to be as compact as possible, with the minimum of sinuosities; 'natural geographic barriers' were not to be crossed, especially water bodies such as Lake Washington and Puget Sound, and the crest of the Cascade Mountains. As far as possible the new districts were to reflect some units of character or interest. In particular Indian reservations should not be split between two districts and as much as possible of Seattle central area (i.e. the black ghetto) was to be within one district. Morrill also noted that he seemed to be expected to meet these criteria by changing the existing structure as little as possible. Presumably this was to avoid confusion in the minds of the electors and the protests that would arise from incumbent legislators and parties which would have to reorganize their local branches to accord with the new districts. Finally, he was instructed to avoid contact with the press and all political figures, and to ignore the location of representatives' homes and considerations of party political power. Interested parties could, however, submit representations. He was given one month to complete the task.

Morrill had originally hopes to use one of the existing computer programs, but with 2000 space units to deal with time available was too short for the necessary adaptations. So he used 'a manual, somewhat intuitive, patient experimental approach' (p. 472). Of all the criteria he was given he managed to observe most strictly the 1 per cent rule of maximum population deviation and compactness, although the effort to preserve the population rule did result in some rather sinuous districts. He was also compelled to divide fifteen counties, but placed the divisions in sparsely populated areas, away from local centres. Some water crossings were also unavoidable since some counties crossed Puget sound. In preserving areas of homogeneous character Morrill had hoped to apply ideas on formal and functional regions. This proved difficult because of the other constraints, but the Indian and Negro areas were not split between several districts. In the rural areas some approximation to nodal regions was possible, and in urban areas many districts were both reasonably nodal and also homogeneous in socio-economic and residential character. Finally, Morrill noted somewhat ruefully that his plan was conservative in that it did not involve radical change in the existing pattern of districts; this feature was criticized by some observers.

Gudgin and Taylor (1974) point out that while studies of area and boundary manipulation have a long tradition, the lack of a simple relationship between seats and votes also arises from the differential concentration of the proportions of party voters among constituencies. They suggest that these differing distributions may be related to probability models and that the causes of electoral bias may be revealed in the variance, skewness, and kurtosis of these distributions, particularly the differing forms of skewness. Applying these ideas to twentieth-century British elections, and in particular to the development of the Labour Party from a regionally concentrated minor party into one of two main national parties, they found evidence to suggest a four- or five-stage developmental model of electoral biases, with a party experiencing different forms and degrees of bias at various stages in its history.

Conclusion

The organization of space for purposes of electoral representation is a task which should be of prime concern to the geographer because it is a facet of his traditional interest in region-building (Cope, 1971).

Moreover, the criteria which are used in constructing these areas and boundaries—spatial contiguity, equal electorates or populations, recognition of settlement patterns, accessibility, and special regional interests—are also central to geographical studies. Again, the detection of improprieties by examination of the shape of areas, alignment of boundaries, the spatial distribution of votes, and related social characteristics are all tasks which the geographer, by definition, is best qualified to carry out. Finally, Morrill's work has shown how political geography can become an applied subject, making a significant contribution to this topic of continuing public concern.

2 Aggregate approaches to electoral geography

Introduction

The study of electoral geography was pioneered in France where the work of Siegfried (1913) initiated a strong school of study which has persisted to the present day, most notably in the work of Goguel (1951) and Lancelot (1968). Indeed, so early and vigorous was the work of geographers on French electoral behaviour that for long they have dominated this particular corner of French political studies and their spatial insights and use of cartographic illustrations find a place in almost every study of elections in France, e.g. Williams (1970). The approach has been applied elsewhere in Europe, particularly in Scandinavia, where studies of voting behaviour usually have a strong spatial emphasis (Rantala and Pesonen, 1967; Stehouwer, 1967). Paullen (1932) and Wright (1932), were the first to study the electoral geography of the U.S.A. After these initial efforts, there were only scattered pieces of work (Dean, 1949; Crisler, 1952; Smith and Hart, 1955) until the mid-1960s, when workers as diverse in their conceptual and technical approach as Burghardt (1964), Lewis (1965), Reynolds and Archer (1969), Cox (1969a), McPhail (1971), and Salter and Mings (1972) entered the field. By the early 1970s electoral geography, particularly in America, was one of the most rapidly developing branches of geography and making increasingly significant contributions to the study of political behaviour in general. In the United Kingdom, however, progress was much slower. Despite the fact that one of the earliest published articles on electoral geography dealt with British elections (Krehbiel, 1916), there was a gap of several decades before the next articles appeared (Roberts and Rummage, 1965). After this several more pieces of work appeared, (e.g., Cox, 1968, 1970; Rowley, 1970, 1971), but nevertheless in comparison with France, Scandinavia, and more recently the U.S.A. little has been contributed by geographers to the study of British electoral behaviour. Nor have British political scientists been particularly conscious of the potential value of the geographer's approach. Aside from Cole (1945), Sharpe (1967), and to a limited extent, Butler and Stokes (1970), virtually none has been aware of the spatial dimension in British elections.

The reasons for this are complex. The analysis of voting behaviour is a recent development in British political studies, and electoral geography may merely have shared the inhibitions of all branches of political studies. Traditionally, studies concentrated on the evolution and working of the British constitution, with particular reference to the relative significance and relationships of the Crown, Lords, Commons, Cabinet and Civil Service (e.g. Bagehot, 1867; Mackenzie, 1950; Jennings, 1955; Walker, 1970). Later, pressure groups became a further object for study (e.g. Finer, 1958; Eckstein, 1960). Early studies of the political parties themselves also tended to concentrate on aspects of party leadership, institutions and organization, rather than the nature of their electoral support.

Nor did the nature and outlook of the British parties during the twentieth century encourage a geographical approach to electoral analysis. The Liberals, who have always emphasized regional devolution in their programmes, declined as a major political party after the First World War and despite their recent revival they have yet to regain their former significance. In its earliest days the Welsh and Scottish branches of the Labour Party did advocate Home Rule, and occasionally it was national party policy (Pelling, 1966). In general, however, the Labour Party has emphasized economic and social issues related to the production, possession and distribution of economic resources and these problems are national in their nature and occurrence. Until recently regional issues were regarded as a distraction from the central concern of transforming the economic and social circumstances of the entire country. The Conservative Party has traditionally eschewed regional issues such as devolution and has emphasized patriotism and national unity. Indeed, until recently the official party title included the word 'Unionist' and until the late 1960's the Scottish Conservatives were always known as 'Unionists'. These attitudes were one consequence of the historic Conservative opposition to Irish Home Rule.

Consequently, when studies of British elections did get under way, they were characterized by two themes. One was a concern with electoral law and the operation of the electoral system (e.g. Butler, 1955, 1963). Another was an emphasis on elections as a national event which decided the nature and outlook of the government. The electorate and its behaviour were also studied from the national standpoint. From the beginning, studies stressed national uniformity of voting patterns (e.g. McCallum and Redman, 1947; Nicholas, 1951) and most subsequent studies of individual constituencies have tended to be illustrations of this basic theme (e.g. Birch and Campbell, 1950; Milne and Mackenzie, 1954; Birch, 1959). It was not until the middle and late 1960's that an appreciation of the spatial dimension of British political affairs developed. This may have been due to a realization that recent economic change had effected different regions of the country in different ways or it may have been a reaction against what some regarded as the steadily increasing centralization of political and economic decision-making. The resulting emphasis on region and locality was reinforced by the steady rise of support for the Welsh and Scottish nationalist parties, culminating in their electoral victories of February and October 1974. All these developments suggested that the previous preoccupation with institutions and national uniformity of behaviour had been overtaken by events and increased attention to the spatial dimension would yield fruitful insights.

However, even if the United Kingdom were still totally uniform in terms of electoral behaviour and no regional issues or parties had arisen, it does not follow that a geographical approach to election studies would be invalid.

The areal-structural approach

This approach examines the spatial pattern and structure of voting choice, as revealed by the election results. The statistics released for each constituency after a British election usually include the total number of persons qualified to vote and the number and proportion actually voting (turnout). On this basis non-voting may also be calculated. In addition the absolute and proportional totals gained by each party are given as well as the majority of the victor. The number of spoiled votes is also issued, though little discussed. Places such as Northern Ireland and the Republic of Ireland where a transferable vote is used issue figures for first-preference votes and also for the transfers of votes at each count as candidates are elected or eliminated.

The electoral geographer may use the material in two main ways. First he may simply consider the spatial distribution of seats won by the various parties, usually with the aid of a choropleth map (Kinnear, 1968) or a map of symbols. The value of this approach lies in the fact that it gives clear and rapid insight into the spatial pattern of the major party strongholds. The situation in Scotland after the general Election of February 1974 is a useful illustration. Here the Labour Party won 40 seats, the Conservatives 21, Liberals 3 and Scottish Nationalists 7. The simple choropleth map in Fig. 5 shows the basic pattern of party victories. The strong predominance of the Labour Party is clearly revealed with its major stronghold in the densely populated urban area of the Central Valley and nearby districts, with outliers in Aberdeen North and Caithness and Sutherland. The Conservative strength in

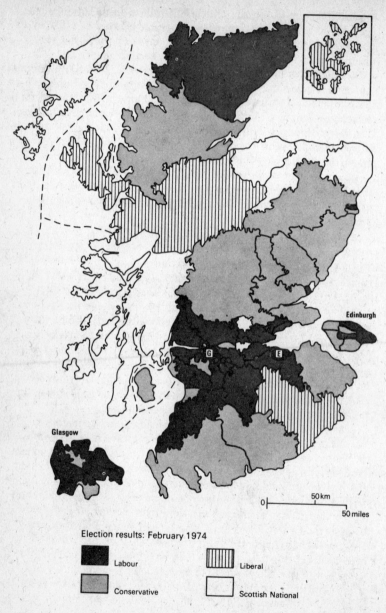

Election results: February 1974

Labour   Liberal

Conservative   Scottish National

FIG. 5 Scotland pattern of party victories in general election, February 1974

suburban Glasgow and Edinburgh and the rural areas of south-western Scotland and the south and south-east Highlands is also clear. The map also serves to emphasize the distribution of the S.N.P. victories along the eastern coast and the isolated nature of the Liberal wins.

The chief disadvantage arising from consideration of outright victories alone is that it does not measure precisely the degree of support for the various parties in each seat. It is quite frequent for the victor to win only a minority of the total votes cast in a constituency and for majorities to be extremely small, in which case discussion on the basis of victory alone fails to register the very fine division of opinions within the constituency. Some striking examples of this are found in south-west England, where there has long been a keen fine-balanced struggle between Conservative, Liberal, and Labour. The situation becomes even more fragmented in some parts of Wales and Scotland, where the nationalist parties are in the field and a four-way split develops. One of the best examples in recent times came in the 1970 election in Ross and Cromarty where the Conservative victor gained slightly less than one-third of the total poll and fewer than 1400 votes separated the three leading contenders (Table 2). Thus it is quite possible for a small transfer of votes in this

TABLE 2
1970 election result: Ross and Cromarty

	Turnout	Percentage of poll
Conservative	6 418	33·2
Liberal	5 617	29·1
Labour	5 023	25·9
Scottish National Party	2 268	11·7
Majority	801	4·1

seat to decide the outcome and the seat may be highly marginal from one election to the next. One method of giving a greater impression of the depth and longevity of electoral behaviour is to present the pattern of party victories over time. Thus the map of election results for the Northern Ireland Parliament 1929–69 (Fig. 8) demonstrates the fact that only a handful of seats ever changed hands, and shows the rigidity and depth of political feeling in that region. Such maps also have a wider application in human geography in that they are useful for regional delimitation. Fig. 7 picks out the regional divide between the Unionists in the central and eastern areas who supported partition of Ireland and wished to maintain the link with the rest of the United Kingdom, and those electors in the western and southern districts who opposed partition and wanted the province to be part of the Irish Republic. Similarly Hart

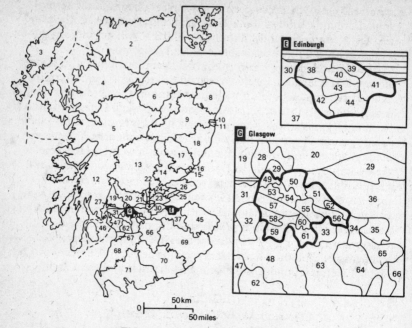

FIG. 6 Scotland: Constituéncies, 1974

1. Orkney and Shetland
2. Caithness and Sutherland
3. Western Isles
4. Ross and Cromarty
5. Inverness
6. Moray and Nairn
7. Banff
8. Aberdeenshire East
9. Aberdeenshire West
10. Aberdeen North
11. Aberdeen South
12. Argyll
13. Kinross and Perthshire West
14. Perth and Perthshire East
15. Dundee West
16. Dundee East
17. Angus South
18. Angus North and Mearns
19. Dunbartonshire West
20. Stirlingshire West
21. Stirling, Falkirk and Grangemouth
22. Clackmannan and Stirlingshire East
23. Dunfermline
24. Fife Central
25. Kirkcaldy
26. Fife East
27. Greenock and Port Glasgow
28. Dunbartonshire Central
29. Dunbartonshire East
30. West Lothian
31. Renfrewshire West
32. Paisley
33. Rutherglen
34. Bothwell
35. Coatbridge and Airdie
36. Lanarkshire North
37. Midlothian
38. Edinburgh-West
39. Edinburgh-Leith
40. Edinburgh-North
41. Edinburgh-East
42. Edinburgh-Pentlands
43. Edinburgh-Central
44. Edinburgh-South

(1967) used the pattern of votes in a number of Presidential elections to help delimit the South in the U.S.A.

It is probably the strength of the minor parties which is most grossly under-represented by discussion of victories alone. Although the Scottish nationalists contested seventy seats in Scotland in February 1974, gaining 21·9 per cent, yet Fig. 5 merely shows the seven seats gained by the S.N.P. and the three taken by the Liberals, and gives no impression of the strength of these parties in the many other seats they contested. A more satisfactory solution, giving a truer picture of the division of support for the various parties in each seat, is to consider the spatial patterns of votes polled in a choropleth map. Fig. 8 shows the level of support for the Scottish nationalists in each Scottish seat in February 1974. It clearly emphasizes the fact that the victories were merely the peaks of a region of above-average support which extends throughout north-western Scot Scotland and includes seats which, though won by other parties, nevertheless contain many S.N.P. voters. It also shows more isolated outposts of support such as Midlothian, East Kilbride, Lanark, and Galloway, and provides a measure of the striking weakness of the Party in the Central Valley, urban areas of Glasgow and Edinburgh, and the Southern Uplands.

The study of electoral geography can also help to identify regions of stress and strain where social and economic changes are under way. The resultant discontent can be expressed in support for a party which articulates and promises redress for these grievances. The rise of Plaid Cymru, the Welsh nationalist party, in the 1960s has been interpreted as a reaction by the traditional Welsh culture area against the threat of anglicization. Scottish nationalism has been viewed as a response to painful structural changes in the Scottish economy (A. H. Taylor, 1973b).

---

45. Berwick and East Lothian
46. Bute and Ayrshire North
47. Ayrshire Central
48. Renfrewshire East
49. Glasgow-Garscadden
50. Glasgow-Maryhill
51. Glasgow-Springburn
52. Glasgow-Provan
53. Glasgow-Kelvingrove
54. Glasgow-Hillhead
55. Glasgow-Central
56. Glasgow-Shettleston
57. Glasgow-Govan
58. Glasgow-Craigton

59. Glasgow-Pollok
60. Glasgow-Queen's Park
61. Glasgow-Cathcart
62. Kilmarnock
63. East Kilbride
64. Hamilton
65. Motherwell
66. Lanark
67. Ayr
58. Ayrshire South
69. Roxburgh, Selkirk and Peebles
70. Galloway
71. Dumfries

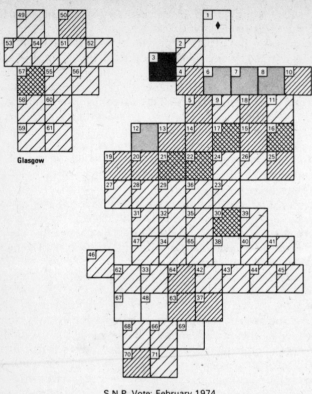

S.N.P. Vote: February 1974

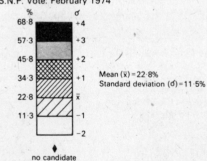

FIG. 7 Scotland: pattern of support for S.N.P. candidates in February 1974
Note: key to constituencies as in Fig. 6.

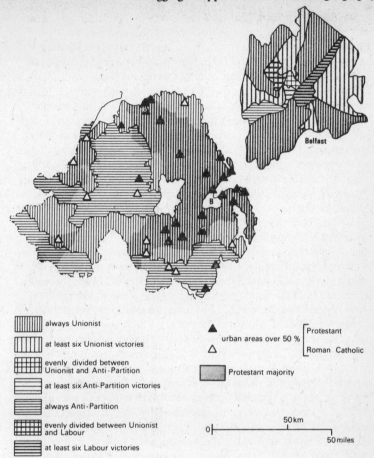

always Unionist

at least six Unionist victories

evenly divided between
Unionist and Anti-Partition

at least six Anti-Partition victories

always Anti-Partition

evenly divided between Unionist
and Labour

at least six Labour victories

▲
△ urban areas over 50 %

⎡Protestant

⎣Roman Catholic

Protestant majority

0   50 km

50 miles

FIG. 8   Northern Ireland: the distribution of religious groups and the pattern of
party victories in Stormont elections 1929–1969

The pattern of support for the S.N.P. in February 1974 (Figs. 5 and 7)
sharply pinpointed the nature and location of some of the grievances
which were at work. Six of the party's seven victories were in northern
coastal areas and, with a few exceptions, the party was best supported
in such littoral districts. The reasons are three. First, several discoveries
of North Sea oil and gas in commercial quantities had recently been
made nearby in offshore drillings and the S.N.P. campaigned vigorously
on Scotland's exclusive rights to the royalties. There was also considerable

public discussion about the need for sites in the North for the construction of oil rigs, the bringing ashore of crude oil, and the installation of
refineries. The possible adverse affects on the physical environment and
on the existing community life in these areas created a good deal of
local unease. Finally, the accession of the United Kingdom to the
European Common Market in 1973 would eventually open all British
inshore waters to fishermen of member countries, and this was an
alarming prospect in these northern areas, where fishing is still a significant element of the local economy. By the recognition and judicious
articulation of these deeply felt grievances, the S.N.P. was able to gain
notable support and victories in this region. Further examples of the
use of electoral statistics to delimit regions of stress and difficulty are
provided by Lewis (1965), who emphasized the use of electoral data in
tracing the course of Negro immigration and the development of the
ghetto area during an inter—censal period in Flint, Michigan, and by
Salter and Mings's discussion (1972) of the relationship between
electoral patterns and Cuban immigration in Miami.

One of the difficulties frequently encountered in the cartographic
representation of electoral behaviour is the variation in size between
urban and rural electoral areas. Thus, in Figs. 5 and 6, Inverness or
Galloway achieved as much, if not more, visual impact as the thirteen
small urban seats of Glasgow. The use of an inset goes some way to
overcome the drawback but it is still not entirely satisfactory. Cotteret
and Emeri (1957) suggested the use of map transformations whereby
each constituency is represented as a square, and the relative location of
the seats and over-all shape of the region under consideration are
preserved as far as possible. The results can sometimes be an unfamiliar
shape, in which an inset is still necessary (Fig. 7), but at least the
problems of variations in shape and area of seats are overcome. It is
possible to introduce further refinements, such as varying the size
of the square according to the winner's majority, or to the proportion
of votes gained by the winning party (Prescott 1959, 1970).

The areal-ecological approach

The brief consideration of the structural approach to electoral geography has already stressed the fact that elections are related to other
aspects of society and culture. In electoral geography there is a long
tradition of viewing election results in relation to the socio-economic
and demographic features of the constituencies in which they occur.
This ecological approach uses aggregate data culled from official
sources such as census reports.

The relationship may be brought out in different ways. One of the most frequently used is the cartographic approach. Maps of the election results are overlaid with or placed close to maps of relevant data, and conclusions drawn from similar spatial distributions. Many valuable insights may be required by this method. For instance, the pattern of party political victories in Northern Ireland elections 1929 to 1969 may be compared with the distribution of religious groups in 1961 (Fig. 8). Clearly the spatial distributions shown closely resemble each other. Unionist sentiment is strongest in the eastern and central areas of the province, with outliers in the north-west. Similarly, the Protestant community is numerically dominant in these areas. Conversely, in those districts with a Catholic majority anti-partition candidates were returned. In his study of Flint, Michigan, Lewis (1965) similarly used cartographic means to show the relationship between income and Republicanism, and between Negro population and Democratic voting.

Electoral geographers, following the general trend in geography, have increasingly used statistical techniques to examine the relationships between voting patterns and socio-economic factors. Various forms of simple correlation analysis have proved valuable in testing hypotheses suggested by visual comparison of maps of electoral returns and socio-economic data. In a study of the Republic of Ireland's Labour Party, Busteed and Mason (1970) first noted that in the 1965 election the party was most strongly supported in the rural areas of the south and south-east. They suggested that this support pattern was related to the distribution of semi-skilled and unskilled rural workers, and tested the hypothesis by correlating first-preference votes against material derived from the 1966 Census of the Republic. A weak positive correlation of 0·54 emerged. To check that there was no relationship with lower-class workers in general, Labour votes were correlated with unskilled and semi-skilled workers in both rural and urban areas. The coefficient of +0·21 confirmed that there was no significant correlation. In the 1969 election, however, it appeared Labour made considerable gains in urban areas, with 9 of its 18 deputies being returned from the Dublin region. The correlation with rural workers was now +0·61 while with rural and urban workers combined it had risen to +0·70. This was accepted as confirmation that in the intervening period there had been a considerable increase in support for Labour in the urban areas. Brunn and Hoffmann (1970) combined the use of both cartographic and correlation techniques in their study of the geography of Negro and white voting on an open-housing referendum in Flint, and Birdsall (1969) used choropleth maps and simple and multiple regression

TABLE 3

Variable input

(all percentages, except distance from London)

RGT6:	total poll gained by Conservatives and other 'right' parties in 1966
LFT6:	total poll gained by Labour and other 'left' parties in 1966
LIB 6:	total poll gained by Liberals in 1966.
TRN6:	turnout in 1966 (as percentage of qualified electors)
DIST:	distance from central London.
SHDW:	households in shared dwelling.
M20	total population aged 20 and over which is male.
F20:	total population aged 20 and over which is female.
PLC6:	total poll gained by Plaid Cymru in 1966.
WLSH:	total population Welsh-speaking in 1961 Census.
A25:	total population aged 25–30.
A30:	total population aged 30–44.
OAP:	total population aged 65 and over.
UNMP	total economically active who are unemployed.
AGRC:	population in employment employed in agriculture.
MING:	population in employment employed in mining.
MNFG:	population in employment employed in manufacturing.
DSTB:	population in employment employed in distribution.
PROF:	economically active population employed as professional workers.
EMPL:	economically active population employed as employers and managers
FSMO:	economically active population employed as foremen, skilled manual workers, and self-employed.
NOML:	economically active population employed as non-manual workers.
PSAG:	economically active population employed as personal service workers, semi-skilled manual workers, and agricultural workers.
UNML:	economically active population employed as unskilled manual workers.
ONOC:	total dwellings owner-occupied.
CNHO:	total dwellings rented from local authority or New Town Corporation.
NO FB:	households without fixed baths.

in his study of the vote for Governor Wallace in the 1968 Presidential election.

Roberts and Rummage (1965) were among the earliest to apply multivariate statistical techniques to electoral grography, using multiple regression with residuals in examining the relationships between the British Labour Vote in 1951 and eleven variables from the 1951 Census, describing aspects of social class, age, education, house tenures, and distance from coalfields. Cox (1968) and McPhail (1971) used factor analysis in their studies of the London Metropolitan Area and Los Angeles. The advantage of such techniques lies in their ability to deal

TABLE 4
Variable loadings on components

| Variable | Components | | | |
	One	Two	Three	Four
RGT	+0·613	+0·680	–	–
LFT	−0·876	–	–	–
LIB	+0·507	–	+0·504	–
TRN	+0·566	–	–	–
DIST	+0·530	−0·529	–	–
SHDW	–	0·515	–	–
M20	−0·702	–	+0·578	–
F20	+0·702	–	−0·577	–
PLC	–	−0·778	–	–
WLSH	–	−0·685	–	–
A25	−0·578	+0·594	–	–
A30	−0·543	–	–	–
OAP	+0·775	–	–	–
UNMP	–	–	−0·564	–
AGRC	+0·547	–	+0·622	–
MING	−0·680	–	–	–
MNFG	−0·750	–	–	–
DSTB	+0·890	–	–	–
PROF	+0·728	–	–	–
EMPL	+0·909	–	–	–
FSMO	−0·524	–	–	–
NOML	+0·575	+0·626	–	–
PSAG	−0·724	–	–	–
UNML	−0·566	–	–	+0·580
ONOC	–	–	−0·552	−0·519
CNHO	–	+0·547	–	+0·503
NOFB	–	−0·749	–	–
Variance	37·42%	20·1%	11·45%	6·95%
Accumulated Value as % Total Variance	37·42%	57·52%	68·97%	75·92%

with a large number of variables and a large number of observations. This is particularly true of factor and principal components analysis where a large array of data is reduced by picking out those groups of variables most closely interrelated. These two techniques are discussed in detail by authorities such as Harman (1967) and King (1969). For present purposes their most useful quality is that the groups of variables ('factors' in factor analysis, 'components' in principal components analysis) are picked out in descending order of importance and their significance in each area or constituency is indicated by a value or 'score'. When the variable input includes electoral statistics, the factors or components which contain the electoral variables may be regarded as those particularly associated with a political viewpoint.

An example of this approach is provided by the application of principal components analysis to material selected from the 1961 and 1966

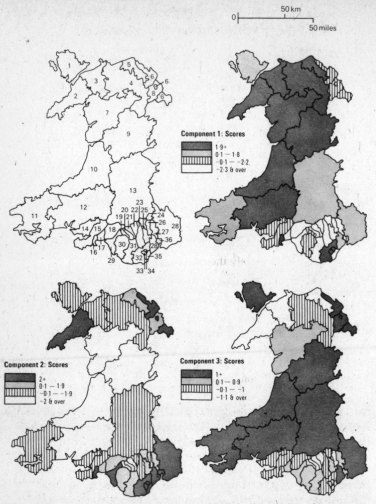

FIG. 9 Wales: pattern of component scores in 1966 election results and census returns

1. Anglesey	10. Cardigan	19. Rhondda West	28. Monmouth
2. Caernarvon	11. Pembroke	20. Rhondda East	29. Aberavon
3. Conway	12. Carmarthen	21. Aberdare	30. Ogmore
4. Denbigh	13. Brecon and Radnor	22. Merthyr Tydfil	31. Pontypridd
5. Flint West	14. Llanelli	23. Caerphilly	32. Barry
6. Flint East	15. Gower	24. Ebbw Vale	33. Cardiff West
7. Merioneth	16. Swansea West	25. Bedwellty	34. Cardiff North
8. Wrexham	17. Swansea East	26. Abertillery	35. Cardiff South East
9. Montgomery	18. Neath	27. Pontypool	36. Newport

census reports and the 1966 general election results in Wales. A total of 27 variables (Table 3) was chosen for each of the 36 constituencies. A simple unrotated principal components analysis was used which arranged the values in a product-moment correlation matrix and derived a total of 27 components from this. For purposes of demonstration and brevity the correlation matrix will not be reproduced here and only components accounting for over 5 per cent of total variance and composed of variables loading 0·5 and over will be discussed and mapped (Table 4. Fig. 9). Component one summarized the variables linked with the main political viewpoints. Amongst those which loaded positively, managerial, professional, and non-manual occupations, old age, and female population were associated with Conservative support, together with agriculture, remoteness and support for Liberalism, suggesting that Liberals and Conservatives were competing for support amongst broadly similar groups. The positive scores were most notable in the rural areas of north and central Wales, with some outliers in the south-central and also the suburban and urban areas of the south-east (Fig. 9). These are certainly the limited areas in Wales where the Conservative can occasionally win seats. Amongst the negative loadings, the Labour vote was associated with manufacturing, males, mining, unskilled and semi-skilled manual workers, and the younger age groups (Table 4). The negative scores were clustered in the south and south-east with a small group in the extreme north-east, and these are the areas with a long tradition of heavy support for Labour.

In component two the most notable positive loadings again described a right-wing vote and non-manual workers, this time also associated with public authority housing and shared dwellings. The positive scores were mostly concentrated in the south and south-east, with a small group in the north-east and also Caernarvon (Fig. 9). Again, most of these are areas with seats which have on occasion been won by the Conservatives. Other seats also score positively on this component, either because there are non-manual or Conservative elements present, though never enough to give a Conservative victory (e.g. Pontypridd, Newport) or because they have notable elements of public authority or shared housing (e.g. Aberavon, Ebbw Vale). The negative loadings describe some elements of the traditional Welsh culture such as Welsh language, remoteness, poorer housing, and support for the nationalist party (Table 4). Negative scores are most notable in rural areas of central, south-central, and North Wales with a notable autlier in a small cluster of inland valley seats in the Rhondda, Aberdare, Menthyr, and Caerphilly district. This pattern is endorsed by the fact that since the mid-1960s Plaid Cymru have polled best and even captured seats in these regions.

Among the positive loadings on component three agriculture and male population are associated with Liberal voting whilst female population, unemployment, and owner-occupation are the most notable negative loadings (Table 4). Positive scores are concentrated in the rural areas of central and southern Wales, with some very scattered outliers in the north, north-east, and south-east (Fig. 9). Certainly areas with a traditionally strong Liberal element such as Montgomery, Merioneth, Anglesey, and Carmarthen do emerge but the inclusion of seats such as Monmouth, Bedwellty, Ogmore, and Swansea East is due to agricultural employment or population structure, since the Liberals are notably weak in these areas. The concentration of negative scores in the far north (Caernarvon, West Flint) and some of the seats of north and west Glamorgan is due to Liberal weakness, or lack of agricultural employment, or high unemployment levels.

This piece of analysis also serves to demonstrate some of the drawbacks inherent in the use of multivariate methods in electoral geography. One of the greatest disadvantages lies in the fact that they must rely on data sources which may not enumerate all the politically relevant elements in a society. One important factor which by its nature cannot be enumerated in Census Reports is political history and tradition. In Wales, for example there has been a long tradition of anti-Conservativatism in politics which has led to strong support for Liberal, Labour, and latterly Plaid Cymru candidates. Equally, Census Reports may not enumerate some of the more tangible cultural variables which may also have political significance. There has been no official enumeration of religious affiliations in Great Britain since 1851, yet it is undeniable that Protestant Nonconformity was a powerful element in Welsh politics in the late nineteenth and early twentieth centuries, serving to reinforce the anti-Conservative and radical tendencies in the Welsh electorate and still surviving in some areas today (Morgan, 1963). Because there were no data for either of these variables they had to be omitted from the exercise, although they probably go a long way towards explaining certain anomalous results of the analysis. Some of the seats such as Caernarvon, Cardigan, and Montgomery which scored heavily positive on component one, summarizing elements which support a Conservative viewpoint, have never been Conservative in the present century, returning instead Liberal, Labour, or Plaid Cymru members. The explanation lies in the fact that these missing variables of tradition and religion have been strong in such areas and have historically been linked with anti-Conservative voting.

Conclusion

The aggregate approaches considered here provided some of the earliest insights into electoral behaviour and still contribute much of value to the subject (e.g. Pelling, 1967). At their simplest they can be easy, quick, and inexpensive studies to carry out, but with the increasing availability of Census data, computation facilities, and package programs, the possible dimensions and technical sophistication of such studies have increased considerably. There has also been a parallel increase in conceptual and methodological rigour. However, there are certain disadvantages in the traditional type of aggregate study. First, the purely structural approach can be somewhat cursory and static. It places the emphasis only on description of the spatial structure of the end result of voting behaviour and ignores or assumes much of the underlying processes. Moreover, the use of aggregate data is itself open to question. The electoral statistics of turnout, spoiled papers, valid votes, party totals, and majority size which are released for each constituency in British elections are in many ways inadequate descriptions of electoral behaviour for study purposes. Each British constituency contains on average over 60 000 electors. Clearly, therefore, any attempt to summarize their political behaviour in these half-dozen statistics involves study at a very generalized level and does considerable violence to the decision-making processes of the individual electors. Further, the attempt to relate aggregate electoral statistics to aggregate Census data always runs the risk of what has been termed the 'ecological fallacy'. This is the error of assuming that ecological correlations at the constituency or district level are also correlations at the individual level. Several workers have pointed out that changes in scale of study can bring about changes in the strength and even the direction of such correlations (Robinson, 1950). Perhaps the role of such aggregate voting studies may be viewed as adding a further dimension to regional analysis by their spatial correlation with other cultural variables and by their very nature as a free expression of personal attitudes. Thus Carter and Thomas (1969) were able to use the results of the 1968 referendum on Sunday opening of licensed premises in Wales, together with data on the Welsh language, to delimit the extent and structure of the traditional Welsh culture area. Second, in studies specifically devoted to electoral geography, the areal-structural or ecological approaches may be used as preliminary stages in larger studies, suggesting relationships or hypotheses which may be tested and accepted, rejected, or modified by the application of other approaches.

3 The behavioural approach to electoral geography

Introduction

In many of its characteristics the behavioural approach to electoral geography represents a reaction against what were felt to be some of the inadequacies of the traditional methods noted earlier. Like the behavioural approach to human geography generally it is essentially process-oriented, examining the stages and processes whereby spatial patterns of location, distribution, and interrelationships arise. As such it concentrates on decision-making, emphasizing the fact that the spatial locations and patterns seen on the map are the end result of a mass of individual decisions and actions. These decisions in turn are made by individuals only after a process of evaluation of the available information about the outside world. Thus behavioural studies are characterized by strong emphasis on the study of information flow. The individual uses the information he receives to construct an image of his environment and, in particular, of the parties and candidates competing for his vote. Here a link with the voluminous body of perception studies in geography is particularly strong. The perceived image is compared with the elector's personal aims and values and his personal political behaviour is the result. He may be still undecided and seek out more information before coming to a decision; he may decide not to vote, out of confusion, apathy, or hostility towards all the competing parties and candidates; or finally, he may vote, and in choosing amongst the candidates he will contribute one point to the over-all spatial pattern of electoral choice.

This is very much a model-oriented approach, seeking to disaggregate not only the spatial structure of voting behaviour but also the stages of the decision-making which produced that structure. It is hardly surprising that it has made a profound impact on electoral geography. Golledge, Brown, and Williamson (1972) pointed out that of all the branches of human geography political geography has traditionally been most concerned with spatial consequences of political and military decisions. This being so, it was natural that the behavioural approach should have its greatest impact on that part of political geography which studies the results of choice between political groups. As the behavioural approach had long been applied to voting studies in political science interdisciplinary diffusion was perhaps merely a matter of time. Electoral geography by its very nature and its position between two disciplines with a common interest in voting, has virtually been transformed by the behavioural approach.

The principles

If the aggregate results of an election as expressed in absolute and percentage figures have been termed 'voting response surfaces', then in behavioural terms the individual elector who will eventually decide whether or not to vote and whom to vote for may be conseptualized as a node or point in an information flow network. The first role which such an individual performs is to receive information. (Cox, 1969b) has pointed out that the information received by an elector may be of various types, ranging from the non-political to the highly political. Politically relevant information can vary from one society to another, depending on the bases of political cleavages. Thus in England the current level of the retail price index is highly relevant politically, while in the U.S.A. the availability of public transport to convey children to distant schools, in order to achieve racial balance in the classrooms, is a political issue. However, as Cox also pointed out, simple information on various issues can have little significance unless the elector is also aware of the policies competing parties and candidates hold on the issue in question. Only when such supplementary facts are available is the elector able to evaluate and choose between the rivals. Supplementary information of this type is clearly highly political in content. It also has a marked partisan bias in that, together with an outline of group policy on an issue, it also seeks actively to commend the group or candidate to the electorate and to encourage electors to vote accordingly.

Such highly partisan pieces of advocacy are termed 'cues'. There are many sources of such cues; the most obvious are the political parties themselves, since at the local level in particular they exist to confirm, mobilize, and extend party support. They may almost be regarded as existing simply to provide cues, presenting party policies and candidates in the most favourable light. Economic interest groups, such as trade unions and employers' associations, also provide cues as they exist to protect and advance the interests of their members and to this end have often developed close links with political parties. Newspapers also frequently have distinctive partisan loyalties of varying intensities. Consequently, they tend to select, present, and interpret news and information in a manner favourable to their political ideals. Cox rightly points out that sources of partisan cues differ from one society to another. In African states tribal groups seem most important whilst in late-nineteenth-century Wales religious denominations were highly significant. The cues in any one state can also vary through time. In nineteenth-century British elections religion and the local peer or landlord were notable sources for cues (Pelling, 1967). This gradually changed until by the mid-twentieth century it was strongly asserted that socio-economic class provided by far the strongest cues (Blondel, 1965). Finally, the spatial extent of cues can also bring a distinctive element into voting patterns. The more localized the origin of a set of cues, then the more likely they will lead to an idiosyncratic element in the over-all national pattern of voting choice. Thus Welsh, Irish, and Scottish nationalism all provide regionally distinctive cues which can ensure the return of some M.P.s to the Westminster Parliament on a distinctive platform of regional self-assertion.

The second role of the node in the network is to process information. It has been rightly pointed out that relatively little attention has been paid to this stage, although it is obvious that is occurs. Too often in studies of information flow it has been assumed that the elector is politically neutral, and is totally open to conviction by the equality, volume, or bias of information directed at him. Other studies have suggested, however, that most people do identify themselves to at least some degree with a political party, and relatively few are either open-minded or indifferent. Consequently, it would seem clear that one of the most significant activities of this stage is the process whereby the elector evaluates information and cues received against his own pre-existing partisan loyalties. Those who are apolitical will ignore political information and cues and very likely will not vote at all. Most electors have certain ideas on how they would ideally like to see society and the state organized, and most have already chosen a party which they believe most likely to achieve these long-term goals. Consequently any information or cues received is measured against these ideals. A few with minority party outlooks, not represented by any of the competing parties, will reject all the information, cues, and candidates and abstain. The majority will compare the information and cues with their aims and may react in various ways. First, it is possible that the information and cues are at variance with the elector's partisan preference. He may simply respond by ignoring unpalatable material. Alternatively, he may accept the information but reinterpret it and superimpose a gloss favourable to his partisan predisposition. Again, he may find his priorities and loyalties shaken by the information and cues from the opposing party. He may reconsider and revise his outlook, eventually either restoring his partisan loyalties or becoming apolitical or even changing his viewpoint. Studies suggest that reconsideration and conversion are rare, but most likely to occur in younger voters or those not strongly identified with their chosen party (Butler and Stokes, 1970).

Finally, the elector may be viewed as a sender of information. Every elector receives and processes information and cues, no matter how apolitical he may be, and every elector is a potential sender. However, some electors are more vigorous and voluminous senders than others, this depending to a certain extent on inherent personality differences and the degree of political involvement and commitment: those who are natural leaders and opinion-formers and those who are politically committed will be more inclined to send relevant information and cues.

Thus far the discussion has been confined to the function of points in the information flow network, with the assumption that all information and cues are equally available everywhere and that there is equal chance everywhere of an elector picking them up. In practice there are several possible sources of bias in a network. Cox (1969b) has listed four. First, distance bias, whereby the probability of an elector picking up data from a source declines with increasing distance between them. The effects of such distance bias are frequently qualified by other variables such as education, sex, and socio-economic status. Acquaintance circle bias suggests that if two individuals belong to the same acquaintance circle, then there is an increased probability of information exchange. The effects of this bias would appear to vary with at least two variables. First the spatial extent of the group catchment area. The more confined these are then the greater the effect of local opinion on electors, since individuals belonging to an organization drawing its membership from a wide area are much more likely to encounter a variety of political information and cues (Cox, 1969a). Second, the degree of interconnection between the members of the group. Rural and small urban areas tend to behave differently from the larger, urban centres (Busteed and Mason, 1970), and this may well be because social organization in such areas is characterized by small, tightly-knit groups with widely accepted values and a very low rate of population change.

The third form of bias is termed 'forced-field', to describe the situation if one of the potential sources of cues has an inherently greater attractiveness for electors than the others. This can involve what has been termed 'homo-political selectivity', the process whereby an elector deliberately searches for those sources of information and cues which he knows will confirm his own partisan outlook. Thus in England, a Conservative is likely to read 'The Daily Telegraph' and, in France, a

Communist will take *L'Humanité*. This of course creates difficulties in studies of information flow. It becomes necessary to decide whether an elector's personal outlook is identical with the partisan bias of his information and cues because they have converted him to that outlook, or whether he was already of that persuasion and chose sources which would reinforce it.

A second factor giving certain sources greater drawing power is their relative status in society, particularly if the social organization is hierarchical and traditional in outlook. In the rural areas and country towns of nineteenth-century England peers and local squires were frequently looked to for a lead on political issues of the day, as they were the leaders of local society. Such persons were also able to operate a system of rewards to encourage and confirm supporters, and sanctions to punish and deter tenants who 'voted wrong' (Pelling, 1967). In nineteenth-century Wales the minister of the Non-Conformist chapel was an attractive source of information and cues. The relative significance of such nodes can alter with changes in society and electoral law, and with the general decline in religious belief, the clerical influence in modern Wales only survives in the remoter parts of the traditional Welsh culture zone (Carter and Thomas, 1969). Again, in early-nineteenth century Ireland the landlord influence on those few of the tenantry who were qualified for the franchise was predictably strong. Then the Catholic Emancipation Act of 1829, which extended the franchise on equal terms to Catholics, together with the rise of an Irish nationalist movement based on the Catholic Church, diminished the drawing power of the landlord and replaced him by the parish priest. The Secret Ballot Act (1872) and the Corrupt and Illegal Practices Act (1883) effectively ended the rewarding and punishment of voters. But the personal influence of individual industrialists, such as the Pilkingtons at St. Helens or landlords like the Derbys in Lancashire, persisted into the present century and could sometimes be sufficient to secure their election or that of their relatives or nominees. Indeed it probably persists in those parts of the world still characterized by rural, small-town, traditionalist, and hierarchical societies.

Finally, reciprocity bias. Where strong, reciprocal relationships exist between two persons or a group of persons, there is a markedly increased probability of constant interchange of information and cues, as it is likely that the views of the persons concerned will be identical and mutually reinforcing.

Operational models of the behavioural approach

Group membership studies consist of identifying relationships between the characteristics of distinct social groups and voting behaviour. Each group considered has at least two characteristics, namely group identity and political outlook as reflected in voting behaviour. In this operational model the group is regarded as an information flow sub-system, the members of the group being 'points' in the information flow network and membership of the group being viewed as linkage with the network. Group voting behaviour is regarded as an expression of group partisan attitudes and a measure of the nature and volume of information and partisan cues circulating within the group. Any area dominated by a distinct partisan outlook will in effect be the scene for an information network in which certain types of information and partisan cues are dominant. The nature and strength of group membership is described by aggregate data derived from census reports and survey analysis, and their political behaviour is described by aggregate election results. The relationships between the two are described by statistical analysis. The groups studied to date within the framework of this conceptual model are socio-economic (Cox, 1968), religious groups (Cox, 1970) and organizational groups (Cox, 1969a).

When an elector moves into an area which already has a marked partisan bias, the *relocation effect* can be invoked to explain his eventual acceptance of the majority view. As he takes up residence and begins to search for formal and informal social contacts the newcomer is most likely to encounter information cues favourable to the dominant party. Persistent bombardment in this fashion will eventually, it is suggested, convert him to the majority viewpoint, thereby further extending the information flow network. Cox (1968) argues that this was the process behind the observed growth of Conservative support in the suburban zones of the London metropolitan area during the 1950s, and suggested that it paralleled a similar growth of Republican strength in the suburban areas of metropolitan America. However, the political conservatism of suburbia is a controversial topic and, as Kasperson pointed out in a commentary on Cox's work (1969), there is a considerable body of American work that questions the converting effect of relocation. Some suggest that the growing suburban Republicanism is due to the in-migration of higher-income groups who are already Republican; others dispute that the Republican upsurge has been as strong as the conversionists say and point to an increased Democratic suburban strength and the electoral marginality of suburban areas. In general it would seem that the relocation effect has been overstated, and the assumption that the incoming resident is politically neutral and open-minded is somewhat naive. However, the workings of the relationships between migration and the precise pattern of political choice (Rowley, 1970) remain to be elucidated.

The *neighbourhood effect* is used to explain the long-observed fact that in certain small areas the actual strength of a party can be much greater than the numerical strength of its natural supporters would lead one to expect. For example, in the mining communities of South Wales support for Labour among the middle classes is much greater than the national average, and in the coast resorts of southern England working-class support for the Conservatives stands at a strikingly high level. Butler and Stokes, in their study of electoral behaviour in Great Britain (1970), argue that there is an observed tendency for the local political environment to produce unexpectedly high levels of support for the locally dominant party. It has been suggested that once the local strength of the dominant party reaches a certain 'tipping point' then it so dominates the local information flow network that those electors who on grounds of class or some other characteristic could be expected to support the opposing party are pulled over to conform to the locally dominant political outlook. Various explanations of this phenomenon have been offered. Some would argue that electors are aware of, and consciously conform to, the local political milieu; others point to the cumulative effect of the local environment as transmitted by informal personal conversation at both work and leisure (Butler and Stokes, 1970; Cox, 1971). The exact workings of such processes remain to be clarified by empirical research, but some tentative suggestions may be carefully framed. Once again the locally dominant group with its distinctive political outlook may be viewed as an information flow network. This time, however, because of its overwhelming numbers its partisan cues can be regarded as virtually monopolizing the local information flow. The effect of this is likely to be greatest on local people growing up in such an environment. For those whose socio-economic background would naturally lead them to conform to the local environment there is no problem. The combined information flow network of both class and locality are pushing them in the same direction. But for those whose socio-economic status links them to an information flow network conveying partisan cues at variance with those of the local milieu, there is a conflict. It would seem likely that, particularly during the formative years of political opinion, the information and partisan cues of the local area would probably be sufficient to fix the elector's partisan preference. Then, when his occupation brings him into contact with novel information and cues his predisposition, plus the continuing partisan nature of the local environment, are sufficient for him to ignore, reject, or reinterpret conflicting data in the manner suggested earlier. In this way the partisan nature of the local network is further extended.

The *friends and neighbours* effect has also been remarked upon in a variety of situations over the years. It describes the situation when a candidate receives higher than average support where he is particularly well known, for example in his birthplace, school, home, or workplace. The distance decay mechanism whereby this personal support declines with increasing distance involves, once again, processes of information transmission. First, a sense of local loyalty and pride in the achievements of a 'local boy made good' would cause many electors to give him their support regardless of his party affiliation. Secondly, this loyalty and identification with the candidate, plus his frequent personal contacts with the electors, ensure the insertion into the network of further information and cues favourable to his candidacy.

The most vigorous attempts to measure the 'friends and neighbours' effect have been made by Johnston (1972, 1973) and Forrest and Johnston (1973) in their studies of local elections in New Zealand. In a study of the 1968 Christchurch City Council elections Johnston found that on average 85 per cent of the spatial variation in a candidate's support could be accounted for by what he termed the *party effect*. In this he subsumed the workings of all the models discussed above and used the term to describe the level of political support common to all the candidates. The remaining 15 per cent comprised 12 per cent random elements and 3 per cent due to the 'friends and neighbours' effect. Johnston found that distinct cones of above average support were discernible around the homes or workplaces of 14 or the 26 candidates who lived inside the city boundary. Another two were actually less popular in such areas than elsewhere in the city—they suffered a negative 'friends and neighbours' effect. There was also some tendency for the personal support of candidates living just outside city boundaries to spill over into those city districts closest to the boundary and to their homes. Johnston tentatively concluded that the 'friends and neighbours' effect seemed to be cyclical, tending to be most important for little-known candidates at the start, and well-known candidates at the end of their careers. He also suggested that the significance of the 'friends and neighbours' effect was greatest at an election when party affiliations were weakest and the mass media coverage of the campaign was at a minimum. Otherwise, party loyalty and blanket media coverage tended to overwhelm the personal and individual effect. Similar conclusions emerged from the Forrest and Johnston study of the 1971 City Council elections in Dunedin (1973), though here the importance of other focal points of personal influence besides the home was stressed. Examination of the 1971 local elections in Christchurch (Johnston, 1974) confirmed that 80 per cent of the variation in candidate performance was accounted for by party effect. Additional support for a candidate on the basis of his local residence and reputation was neither strong nor general. It was most notable for independent candidates and for others who lived in areas where the opposition party was dominant. Where such additional support occurred, it was visible at the polling booths closest to the candidates' homes. It is significant that both Key (1949) and Coleman (1966) suggest that the 'friends and neighbours' effect was restricted to rural and small urban areas, which may go some way towards explaining the disappointingly small percentage of the variation accounted for by this model in such fairly large cities (Christchurch 160 000 residents, Dunedin 107 500).

Finally, there is the *location protection model*, in which the residents of a particular location perceive what they believe to be an imminent threat to their interests. They respond in political terms by the formation of a location-specific mutual protection group or by distinctive voting behaviour. Such distinct voting behaviour can only occur, however, if one of the competing candidates or parties advocates a policy of protection for the threatened group. Moreover, both the policy and the identity of the party and candidate advocating it must be known to the group and the intensity of the threat and the appeal of the candidate's policy must be sufficiently strong to impel them to convert their anxiety into actual voting decisions. The consequences for the electoral map can be disturbing. The existing parties may try to accommodate themselves to such grievances, and the most successful will benefit from the increased support. Alternatively local independent candidates may campaign on this issue alone, sometimes securing election, or perhaps merely disturbing the traditional local electoral pattern.

An interesting example of a localized response to a perceived threat occurred in the British general election of October 1964. Starting in the late 1940s there had been an influx of coloured immigrants into Great Britain from Commonwealth countries such as India, Pakistan, and several of the West Indian islands. This had reached a climax in the late 1950s and early 1960s, when, in response to public disquiet, the Conservative government introduced by the Commonwealth Immigrants Act (1962) a system of entry for holders of Ministry of Labour work vouchers, the issue of which was restricted in total numbers. The immigrants did not settle in a totally random or totally even pattern across the country. Rather, they tended to concentrate in those areas where they knew job vacancies were available and friends and relations were already resident. The regions most affected were West Yorkshire, parts of the London region, and the West Midlands (Peach, 1966, 1968).

For a long time this immigration was not regarded as being of any political significance, but as the 1950s passed the level of immigration and public unease increased. It was reflected at the national level by some members of the Conservative Party, and at the regional and local level by some Conservative Party associations and individual candidates in local elections. The most notable impact, however, was felt in the 1964 general election in Birmingham and the West Midlands. At the national level there was a swing of 3·1 per cent from Conservative to Labour, with the Conservatives losing a net total of 62 seats, and Labour gaining a net total of 57 and going on to form the first Labour Government in Britain since 1950. In the West Midlands, however, the pattern was different. While Labour did gain four seats and several others swung to the Party, the over-all characteristic of the region was a below average swing. In several seats, most notably in the north of Birmingham and in the Black Country north-west of the city, there was a movement *against* the national trend from Labour to Conservative (Fig. 10). This culminated in the actual gain of two seats from Labour by the Conservatives.

Investigation (Foot, 1965) showed that these results were due to two factors. First the West Midlands region, as noted earlier, was one of those especially affected by coloured immigration, and it is perhaps hardly surprising that electoral consequences should be felt there. However, this does not explain the absence of similar events in other parts of the country or the fact that in some constituencies in the West Midlands the movement to Labour was close to or above the antional average, and that Labour managed to gain three seats in Birmingham and one nearby. The explanation lies in the political attitudes of the parties, both nationally and locally, and the electors' realization of these policies. The Immigration Act of 1962 had been passed by a Conservative government and opposed by the Labour opposition. This fact alone was sufficient to indicate the general trend of the parties' thinking at the time. At the local Constituency Association level, however, several Conservative candidates developed a vigorous anti-immigrant attitude, arguing for such additional measures as a further reduction in immigration, a total ban, or repatriation of all immigrants already in Britain. Investigation (Deakin 1965; Foot, 1965) showed that the Conservative candidates in Smethwick, Birmingham Perry Bar, and Selly Oak campaigned on anti-immigrant policies, while others either refrained from raising the issue or, as in Birmingham Hall Green and Handsworth, were well known for their liberal views on the subject. This goes some way to explain the swing to Labour in others, but it still does not explain seats such as Birmingham Ladywood, Wednesbury, or Wolverhampton South-East, where, in spite

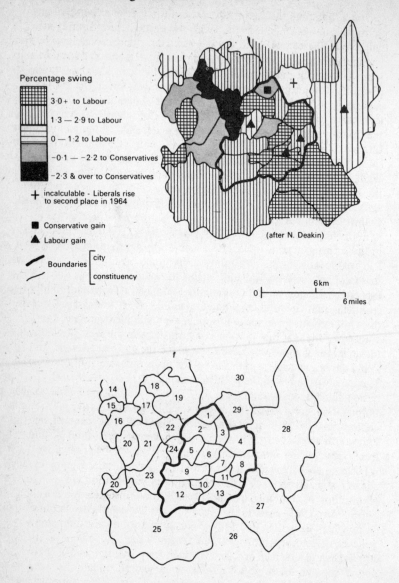

Percentage swing

3·0 + to Labour

1·3 — 2·9 to Labour

0 — 1·2 to Labour

−0·1 — −2·2 to Conservatives

−2·3 & over to Conservatives

+ incalculable - Liberals rise
to second place in 1964

■ Conservative gain

▲ Labour gain

Boundaries [city
              constituency

(after N. Deakin)

0   6 km
0   6 miles

FIG. 10 The West Midlands: patterns of political behaviour in the 1964 general election

of the refusal to raise the immigration issue, there was either a swing to Conservatives or only a below-average swing to Labour. It has been suggested that while candidates themselves may have refrained from raising the issue, their helpers and canvassers may have raised it on the doorsteps, or that anti-immigrant organizations may have been active in some areas, without either the knowledge or the consent of the candidates concerned.

In this example, the perceived threat was coloured immigration, particularly the real or imagined life-style and numbers of those who had already arrived or might come in the near future. At the national level the two chief competing parties took contrasting positions. These contrasts still had to be conveyed to the individual electors at the local level by the supply of information and cues and it is at this point that the contrasting attitudes of individual Conservative candidates and the activities of canvassers and anti-immigrant organizations become important. They may be viewed as the source of cues, raising the issue of immigration as a threat to living standards, life-styles, property values, and physical safety, suggesting that the Labour candidate was unaware, indifferent, or too liberal on the issue, and encouraging support for the Conservative candidate. This explained why, as several observers have pointed out, there was no clear positive relationship between the absolute or relative total of immigrants or overcrowding, or quality of housing on the one hand, and the depth of anti-immigrant feeling and the movement against Labour on the other. These depended upon the attitudes and activities of local sources of information and cues.

The voting response surface, described by aggregate electoral statistics, is the sum total of all the processes envisaged in the models discussed

Key to FIG. 10 opposite

1. Birmingham—Perry Barr	16. Bilston
2. Birmingham—Handsworth	17. Wednesbury
3. Birmingham—Aston	18. Walsall North
4. Birmingham—Stechford	19. Walsall South
5. Birmingham—All Saints	20. Dudley
6. Birmingham—Ladywood	21. Rowley, Regis and Tipton
7. Birmingham—Small Heath	22. West Bromwich
8. Birmingham—Yardley	23. Oldbury and Halesowen
9. Birmingham—Edgbaston	24. Smethwick
10. Birmingham—Selly Oak	25. Bromsgrove
11. Birmingham—Sparkbrook	26. Stratford
12. Birmingham—Northfield	27. Solihull
13. Birmingham—Hall Green	28. Meriden
14. Wolverhampton North East	29. Sutton Coldfield
15. Wolverhampton South West	30. Lichfield and Tamworth

above, plus random factors of the type noted by Johnston (1973) and Forrest and Johnston (1973). The relative importance of these processes is difficult to gauge for various reasons. First, the sheer novelty of the behavioural approach to electoral geography means that so far there is little empirical research conducted within this framework on which valid generalizations can be made with any confidence. Findings to date are derived from Cox's studies on the U.S.A. and those of Johnston and Forrest and Johnston on New Zealand. Second, it must be recalled that while every society contains cleavages and groups within which these processes may operate, the dominant form of grouping varies from one country to another. In the United Kingdom it has long been argued that social class based on occupation is the most important division, while in Canada it is the French/English cultural divide. Third, it should also be borne in mind that while one particular type of group membership may be the national norm, in some regions a varying group may be dominant. Thus, while socio-economic class may indeed be the dominant group over-all in the United Kingdom, in some parts of Wales and Scotland nationality provides a basis for grouping which is at least equally strong. Similarly, in the U.S.A. socio-economic class and ethnic origin compete as the most significant basis for social groups, though locational, neighbourhood, and sectional interests may be more important in smaller cities (Cox, 1971). Finally, the relative significance of various sources of information and cues may change with time and in response to changing circumstances, and produce changes in the spatial patterns of voting behaviour. Barnett (1973) in his study of the diffusion of support for the Danish Communist Party, used a variance component model on election results over the period 1920–64 to investigate the significance of information and cues at the national, regional, and constituency levels, in accounting for the total variability of the pattern of voting responses. He found that during the earliest part of the period localized constituency sources were most significant, comprising factors such as the location of the candidate's home. As time passed, however, the constituency component decreased in importance relative to the national component. After 1945 this consistently accounted for 70 per cent of the total variance. The regional component remained stable throughout the period, usually accounting for 10–15 per cent.

Operationalization of the behavioural approach has relied on two sources, namely aggregate data and survey material. In using aggregate data workers have sought once again to relate electoral returns to census material, but this time the approach, although similar in techniques, has been rethought within the framework of the behavioural principles.

Statistics describing socio-economic groups and election results are not regarded as stating that each individual in a group voted in a particular way. Instead the approach is to regard the statistics as descriptive of the most significant reference groups for sources of information and cues, with the election returns revealing the partisan bias of the cues which are conveyed. The great difficulty of course comes in the fact that workers using this approach can easily slip into the old ecological fallacy of viewing ecological correlates as descriptive of individual behaviour. Survey analysis, involving the compilation of a questionnaire and the interviewing of a sample of electors, does not encounter such difficulties. Indeed, considering the basic postulates of the behavioural approach, it would seem the most appropriate way of investigating all the various stages of information transmisson, reception, processing, decision-making, and electoral choice. But survey analysis is time-consuming and expensive to ogranize, and this may partly explain why it has been relatively little used in electoral geography to date.

Conclusion

Electoral studies comprise the most actively developing aspect of political geography. They have brought the behavioural approach and quantitative techniques into that branch of geography which for long seemed least influenced by recent developments in the general field of human geography. Indeed, electoral geography is now one of the main sources of fresh insights into the general field of human spatial behaviour (Golledge *et al.*, 1972). This, of course, is hardly surprising when one considers that the geography of electoral choice involves a phenomenon which by definition follows on from a process of information flow, processing, and individual choice between competing alternatives. As such, the behavioural approach is instrumental in bringing political geography into line with those other branches of the subject such as migration, consumer behaviour, diffusion studies, and industrial location where behavioural studies are also making a significant impact.

4 General conclusion

Until recently electoral geography, particularly in the British Isles, has been a neglected aspect of the discipline. Gradually it has been realized that geography is profoundly affected by governments and elections, and that electoral statistics are a useful supplementary source of data for human geography as a whole. Furthermore, with the development of political awareness in the discipline (e.g. Smith and Prince, 1971), and the rapid growth of the behaviouralist theme, geographers have realized that their emphasis on spatial locations, distribution, and inter-relationships is particularly well suited to studies of the spatial organiz-ation of representative areas, the processes of political information diffusion and electoral choice, and the spatial structure of the behaviour patterns which result. In this sense perhaps electoral geography is one of the branches of the subject most relevant to current social, economic, and political issues.

Much work remains to be done. Local elections have received relatively little attention (Rowley, 1965, 1971), and practically no survey work has been undertaken by electoral geographers in the United Kingdom. There is also considerable scope for study of the diffusion of support for new parties (A. H. Taylor, 1973); the effects of different schemes of constituency boundaries on election results; information reception and assessment during campaigns; and the much disputed relationship between population change and politcal behaviour. Research along these lines within the behavioural framework and relying mostly on survey analysis would seem to be the most fruitful directions of progress.

References

Allen. A. J. (1964). *The English Voter*. English Universities Press, London.

Bagehot, W. (1867). *The English Constitution*. Longmans, London.

Barnett, J. R. (1973). 'Scale Components in the Diffusion of the Danish Communist Party, 1920–64', *Geographical Analysis* **5**, 35–44.

Birch, A. H. (1959). *Small-Town Politics*. O.U.P., London.

Birch, A. H. and Campbell, P. (1950). 'Voting Behaviour in a Lancashire constituency'. *British Journal of Sociology*, **1**, 197–208.

Birdsall, S. A. (1969). 'Preliminary Analysis of the 1968 Wallace Vote in the Southeast', *Southeastern Geographer*, **9**, 55–66.

Brunn, S. D., and Hoffmann, W. L. (1970). 'The Spatial Response of Negroes and Whites Toward Open Housing: The Flint Referendum', *Annals, Association of American Geographers*, **60**, 18–36.

Burghardt, A. F. (1964). 'The Bases of Support for Political Parties in Burgeland', *Annals, Association of American Geographers*, **54**, 372–90.

Bushman, D. O., and Stanley, W. R. (1971). 'State Senate Reapportionment in the Southeast', *Annals, Association of American Geographers*, **61**, 654–70.

Busteed, M. A. (1974). *Northern Ireland*. Oxford University Press, London.

—— and Mason, H. L. (1970). 'Irish Labour in the 1969 Election', *Political Studies*, **18**, 373–79.

———— (1974). 'The 1973 General Election in the Irish Republic', *Irish Geography*, **7**, 97–106.

Butler, D. E. (1955). 'The Redistribution of Seats', *Public Administration*, **55**, 125–47.

—— (1963). *The Electoral System in Britain since 1918*. Oxford University Press, London.

—— and Stokes, D. (1970). *Political Change in Britain: Forces Shaping Electoral Choice*. Macmillan, London.

Carter, H., and Thomas, J. G. (1969). 'The Referendum on the Sunday Opening of licensed premises in Wales as a criterion of a Culture Region', *Regional Studies*, **3**, 61–71.

Chapman, K. (1971). 'Conservative Policies for the Regions', *Area*, **3**, 8–12.

Chisholm, M. and Manners, G. (1971). *Spatial Policy Problems of the British Economy*. Cambridge University Press.

Chubb, B. (1970). *The Government and Politics of Ireland*. Oxford University Press, London.

Cole, M. (1945). *The General Election of 1945 and after,* **Fabian Research Series,** 102. Fabian Society, London.

Congressional District Atlas of the United States (biannual). U.S. Department of Commerce, Bureau of Census, Washington

Congressional District Data Book (biannual). U.S. Department of Commerce, Bureau of Census, Washington

Cope, C. R. (1971). 'Regionalisation and the Electoral Districting Problem', *Area,* **3,** 190–95.

Cotteret, J. -M., and Emeri, C. (1957). 'Essai de representation des forces politiques', *Revue française de science politique,* 7, 594–625.

Cox, K. R. (1970). 'Geography, Social Contexts and Welsh Voting Behaviour 1861–1951', in Rokkan, S., and Allardt, E. (eds.), *Mass Politics: Studies in Political Sociology.* Free Press, New York.

—— (1971). 'The Spatial Components of Urban Voting Response Surfaces', *Economic Geography,* **47,** 27–35.

—— (1969a). 'The Spatial Structuring of Information Flow and Partisan Attitudes', in Doggan, M., and Rokkan, S. (eds.), *Quantitative Ecological Analysis in the Social Sciences.* M.I.T. Press, Cambridge, Mass., U.S.A.

——(1969b). 'The Voting Decision in a Spatial Context', in Board, C., Chorley, R. J., and Haggett, P. (eds.), *Progress in Grography,* **1,** 81–117, Arnold, London.

—— (1968). 'Suburbia and Political Behaviour in the London Metropolitan Area: 1950–51', *Annals, Association of American Geographers,* **58,** 111–127.

Craig, F. W. S. (1971). *British Parliamentary Election Results, 1950– 1970.* Political Reference Publications, Chichester.

Crisler, R. M. (1952). 'Voting Habits in the United States', *Geographical Review,* **42,** 300–301.

Deakin, N. (1965). *Colour and the British Electorate 1964: six case studies.* Pall Mall, London.

Dean, V. K. (1949). 'Geographical Aspects of the Newfoundland Referendum', *Annals, Association of American Geographers,* **39,** 70–77.

Eckstein, H. (1960). *Pressure Group Politics.* Allen and Unwin, London.

Finer, S. E. (1958). *Anonymous Empire.* Pall Mall, London.

Foot, P. (1965). *Immigration and Race in British Politics.* Penguin, Harmondsworth.

Forrest, E. (1965). 'Electronic Reapportionment Mapping', *Data Processing Magazine.*

Forrest, J., and Johnston, R. J. (1973). 'Spatial Aspects of Voting in Dunedin City Council Elections of 1971', *New Zealand Geographer,* 29, 166–81.

Goguel, F. (1951). *Géographie des elections françaises de 1870 à 1951.* Armand Colin, Paris.

Golledge, R. G., Brown, L. A., and Williamson, F. (1972). 'Behavioural Approaches in Geography: An Overview', *Australian Geographer*, **12**, 59–79.

Gudgin, G., and Taylor, P. J. (1974). 'Electoral Bias and the Distribution of Party Voters', *Transactions, Institute of British Geographers*, **63**, 53–74.

Haggett, P. (1969). 'New Regions for Old', *The Geographical Magazine*, **42**, No. 3, 210–17.

Hale, M. Q. (1965). *Representation and Reapportionment.* Ohio State University Political Studies, 2. Columbus, Ohio.

Harman, H. H. (1967). *Modern Factor Analysis.* University of Chicago Press, Chicago.

Hart, J. F. (1967). *The South-Eastern United States.* Van Nostrand, Princeton.

Jennings, I. (1957). *Parliament.* C.U.P., London.

Johnston, R. J. (1974). 'Local Effects in Voting at a Local Election', *Annals, Association of American Geographers*, **64**, 418–29.

—— (1972). 'Spatial elements in Voting Patterns at the 1968 Christchurch City Council Election', *Political Science*, **24**, 49–61.

—— (1973). 'Spatial Patterns and Influences on Voting in Multi-Candidate Elections: The Christchurch City Council Elections, 1968', *Urban Studies*, **10**, 69–81.

Kasperson, R. E. (1969). 'On Suburbia and Voting Behaviour', Commentary, *Annals, Association of American Geograhers*, **59**, 405–411.

Key, V. O. (1949). *Southern politics in State and Nation.* Random House, New York.

King, L. J. (1969). *Statistical Analysis in Geography.* Prentice Hall, Englewood Cliffs, New Jersey.

Kinnear, M. (1968). *The British Voter: An Atlas and Survey since 1885.* Batsford, London.

Krehbiel, E. (1916). 'Geographical Influences in British Elections', *Geographical Review*, **2**, 419–32.

Lancelot, A. (1968). *L'Abstentionnisme électoral en France,* Cahiers, Foundation Nationale des Sciences Politiques, 162. Paris.

Laux, H. D., and Simms, A. (1973). 'Parliamentary Elections in West Germany: the Geography of Electoral Choice', *Area*, **5**, 161–71.

Le Lohé, M., and Spiers, M. (1964). 'Pakistanis in the Bradford Municipal Elections of 1963', *Political Studies*, **12**, 85–92.

Lewis, P. F. (1965). 'Impact of Negro Migration on the Electoral Geography of Flint, Michigan, 1932–62: a Cartographic Analysis', *Annals, Association of American Geograhers*, **55**, 1–25.

Lewis, P. W., and Skipworth, G. E. (1966). *Some Geographical and Statistical Aspects of the Distribution of Votes in Recent General Elections.* No. 3, Miscellaneous Series, University of Hull, Department of Geography.

Lipset, S. M. (1960). *Political Man*. Doubleday, New York.

Mackenzie, K. (1950). *The English Parliament*. Pelican, Harmondsworth.

McCallum, R. B. and Redman, A. (1947). *The British General Election of 1945*. Oxford University Press, London.

McPhail, I. R. (1971a). 'Recent Trends in Electoral Geography', *Proceedings of the Sixth New Zealand Geography Conference*, 1, 7–12. New Zealand Geographical Society, Conference Series, No. 6, Christchurch.

—– (1971b). 'The Vote for Mayor in Los Angeles in 1969', *Annals, Association of American Geographers*, 61, 744–58.

Manners, G., Keeble, D., Rodgers, B., and Warren, K. (1972). *Regional Development in Britain*. John Wiley, London.

Mills, G. (1967), 'The Determination of Local Government Boundaries', *Operational Research Quarterly*, 18, 243–55.

Milne, R. S., and Mackenzie, H. C. (1954). *Straight Fight*. Hansand Society for Parliamentary Government, London.

Morgan, K. O. (1963). *Wales in British Politics 1868–1922*. University of Wales Press, Cardiff.

Morrill, R. L. (1973). 'Ideal and Reality in Reapportionment', *Annals, Association of American Geographers*, 63, 463–77.

Nagel, S. (1965). 'Simplified Bipartisan Computer Redistricting', *Stanford Law Review*, 17, 863–89.

Nicholas, H. G. (1951). *The British General Election of 1950*. Macmillan, London.

Parker, A. J. (1972). 'Ireland: a consideration of the 1971 Census of Population', *Area*, 4, 31–7.

Paullin, C. O. (1932). *Atlas of the Historical Geography of the United States*. American Geographical Society, New York.

Peach, G. C. K. (1966). 'Factors affecting the Distribution of West Indians in Great Britain', *Transactions, Institute of British Geographers*, 38, 151–63.

—– (1968). *West Indian Migration to Britain*: a Social Geography. Oxford University Press, London.

Pelling, H. (1967). *The Social Geography of British Elections 1885– 1910*. Macmillan, London.

Pelling, H. (1966). *The Origins of the Labour Party 1880–1900*. Oxford University Press, London.

Prescott, J. R. V. (1970). 'Electoral Studies in Political Geography', in Kasperson, R., and Minghi, J. V. (eds.), *The Structure of Political Geography*, 376–83. University of London Press, London.

—– (1972). *Political Geography*. Methuen, London.

—– (1959). 'The Functions and Methods of Electoral Geography', *Annals, Association of American Geographers*, 49, 296–304.

—– (1968). *The Geography of State Policies*. Hutchinson, London.

Prince, H. C. and Smith, D. M. (1971). 'America! America? Views on a Melting Pot: 1. Questions of Social Relevance; 2. Radical Geography —the Next Revolution?' *Area*, 3, 150–7.

Putman, R. (1966). 'Political Attitudes and the Local Community', *American Political Science Review*, **50**, 640–54.

—– and Pesonen, P. (1967). 'Current Election Studies in Finland', *Scandinavian Political Studies*, **2**, 284–94.

Reynolds, D. R., and Archer, J. C. (1969). *An Inquiry into the Spatial Basis of Electoral Geography*. Department of Geography, University of Iowa Discussion Paper No. 11.

Roberts, M. C., and Rummage, K. W. (1965). 'The Spatial Variations in Urban Left-Wing Voting in England and Wales in 1951', *Annals, Association of American Geographers*, **55**, 161–78.

Robinson, W. G. (1950). 'Ecological Correlations and the Behaviour of Individuals', *American Sociological Review*, **15**, 351–57.

Rowley, G. (1970). 'Elections and Population Changes', *Area*, **3**, 13–18.

—– (1965). 'The Greater London Council Elections of 1964: some Geographical Considerations', *Tijdschrift voor Economische en Sociale Geografie*, **56**, 113–14.

—– (1971). 'The Greater London Council Elections of 1964 and 1967: a Study in Electoral Geography', *Transactions, Institute of British Geographers*, **53**, 117–31.

Russett, B. M. (1967). *International Regions and the International System: a Study in Political Ecology*. Rand McNally, Chicago.

Salter, P. S., and Mings, R. C. (1972). 'The Projected Impact of Cuban Settlement on Voting Patterns in Metropolitan Miami, Florida', *Professional Geographer*, **24**, 123–31.

Sharpe, L. J. (ed.). (1967). *Voting in Cities*. Macmillan, London.

Siegfried, A. (1913). *Tableau politique de la France de l'ouest*. Armand Colin, Paris.

Silva, R. C. (1965). 'Reapportionment and Redistricting', *Scientific American*, **213**, 20–7.

Smith, H. R., and Hart, J. F. (1955). 'The American Tariff Map', *Geographical Review*, **45**, 327–46.

Stehouwer, J. (1967). 'Long-Term Ecological Analysis of Electoral Statistics in Denmark', *Scandinavian Political Studies*, **2**, 94–116.

Taylor, A. H. (1973a). 'Journey Time, Perceived Distance and Electoral Turnout—Victoria Ward, Swansea', *Area*, **5**, 59–62.

– (1973b). 'The Electoral Geography of Welsh and Scottish Nationalism', *Scottish Geographical Magazine*, **89**, 44–52.

– (1973c). 'The Spread of Labour Party Candidature for Parliamentary Elections in the East Midlands and South Yorkshire', *The East Midland Geographer*, **5**, 373–79.

Taylor, P. J. (1973). 'Some Implications of the Spatial Organization of Elections', *Transactions, Institute of British Geographers*, **60**, 121–36.

The Times Guide to the House of Commons (after each General Election).

Vale, V., (1969). 'The Computer as Boundary Commissioner?', *Parliamentary Affairs*, **22**, 240–49.

Walker, P. G. (1970). *The Cabinet*. Jonathan Cape, London.

Weaver, J. B., and Hess, S. W. (1963). 'A Procedure for Nonpartisan Redistricting: Development of Computer Techniques', *Yale Law Journal*, 73, 288–308.

Williams, P. (1970). *French Politicians and Elections 1951–69*. Cambridge University Press.

Wright, J. K. (1932). 'Voting habits in the United States: a Note on Two Maps', 22, Geographical Review, 666–72.